By Sir Arthur Quiller-Couch

On the Art of Writing

On the Art of Reading

Studies in Literature
(first series)

Studies in Literature
(second series)

Adventures in Criticism

Charles Dickens and Other
Victorians

Charles Dickens
And Other Victorians

Charles Dickens

And Other Victorians

By

Sir Arthur Quiller-Couch, M.A.

Fellow of Jesus College
King Edward VII Professor of English Literature
in the University of Cambridge

G. P. Putnam's Sons
New York & London
The Knickerbocker Press
1925

Made in the United States of America

PREFACE

ALL save one of the papers here collected were written as lectures and read from a desk at Cambridge; the exception being that upon Trollope, contributed to *The Nation and the Athenaeum* and pleasantly provoked by a recent edition of the "Barsetshire" novels. To these it almost wholly confines itself. But a full estimate of Trollope as one of our greatest English novelists—and perhaps the raciest of them all—is long overdue, awaiting a complete edition of him. His bulk is a part of his quality: it can no more be separated from the man than can Falstaff's belly from Falstaff. He will certainly come to his own some day, but this implies his coming with all his merits and all his defects: and this again cannot happen until some publisher shows enterprise. The expensive and artificial vogue of the three-volume-novel did wonders for Trollope in one generation, to kill him for another: since no critic can talk usefully about books to many of which his hearers have no access. But we shall see Trollope reanimated.

The papers on Dickens and Thackeray attempt judgment on them as full novelists. Those on Disraeli and Mrs. Gaskell merely take a theme, and try to show how one theme, taking possession, will work upon two very different minds. Much more could have been said generally upon both authors, and generically upon the "idea" of a novel.

Preface

As usual, with a few corrections, I leave these lectures as they were written and given, at intervals and for their purpose. They abound therefore with repetitions and reminders which the reader must try to forgive.

ARTHUR QUILLER-COUCH.

January 5, 1925.

CONTENTS

Charles Dickens
and Other Victorians

DICKENS (I)

I

IF anything on this planet be great, great things have happened in Westminster Hall: which is open for anyone, turning aside from London's traffic, to wander in and admire. Some property in the oak of its roof forbids the spider to spin there, and now that architects have defeated the worm in beam and rafter it stands gaunt and clean as when William Rufus built it: and I dare to say that no four walls and a roof have ever enclosed such a succession of historical memories as do these, as no pavement—not even that lost one of the Roman Forum—has been comparably trodden by the feet of grave men moving towards grave decisions, grand events.

The somewhat cold interior lays its chill on the imagination. A romantic mind can, like the spider, spin its cobwebs far more easily in the neighbouring Abbey, over the actual dust to which great men come—

> Here the bones of birth have cried—
> "Though gods they were, as men they died."
> Here are sands, ignoble things
> Dropt from the ruin'd sides of kings.

But in the Abbey is *finis rerum*, and our contemplation there the common contemplation of mortality which, smoothing out place along with titles, degrees and even deeds, levels the pyramids with the low mounds of a country churchyard and writes the same moral over Socrates as over our Unknown Soldier—*Vale, vale, nos te in ordine quo natura permittet sequamur*. In Westminster Hall (I am stressing this with a purpose) we walk heirs of events in actual play, shaping our destiny as citizens of no mean country: in this covered rood of ground have been compacted from time to time in set conflict the high passions by which men are exalted to make history. Here a king has been brought to trial, heard and condemned to die; under these rafters have pleaded in turn Bacon, Algernon Sidney, Burke, Sheridan. Here the destinies of India were, after conflict, decided for two centuries. Through that great door broke the shout, taken up, reverberated by gun after gun down the river, announcing the acquittal of the Seven Bishops.

II

So, if this tragic comedy we call life be worth anything more than a bitter smile: if patriotism mean anything to you, and strong opposite wills out of whose conflict come great issues in victory or defeat, the arrest, the temporary emptiness of Westminster Hall—a sense of what it has seen and yet in process of time may see—will lay a deeper solemnity on you than all the honoured dust in the Abbey.

But, as men's minds are freakish, let me tell you of a solitary figure I see in Westminster Hall more vividly even than the ghosts of Charles I and Warren Hastings bayed around by their accusers: the face and figure of a youth, not yet twenty-two, who has just bought a copy of the Magazine containing his first appearance in print as an author. "I walked down to Westminster Hall," he has recorded, "and turned into it for half an hour, because my eyes were so dimmed with joy and pride that they could not bear the street and were not fit to be seen there."

Now the paper which opened the fount of these boyish tears (here, if you will, is bathos) was entitled *A Dinner at Poplar Walk*. You may find it to-day under another title, "Mr. Minns and his Cousin" among *Sketches by Boz:* reading it, you may pronounce it no great shakes; and anyhow you may ask why anyone's imagination should select this slight figure, to single it out among the crowd of ghosts. Well, to this I might make simple and sufficient answer, saying that the figure of unbefriended youth, with its promise, a new-comer alone in the market-place, has ever been one of the most poignant in life, and, because in life, therefore in literature. Dickens himself, who had been this figure and remembered all too well the emotion that choked its heart, has left us a wonderful portrait-gallery of these lads. But indeed our literature—every literature, all legend, for that matter—teems with them: with these youngest brothers of the fairy-tales, these Oedipus's, Jasons, these Dick Whittingtons, Sindbads, Aladdins, Japhets in search of their Fathers; this Shakespeare holding horses for a groat, that David comely from the sheepfold with the basket of loaves and cheeses. You remember De Quinccy and the stony waste of Oxford Street? or the forlorn and invalid boy in Charles Lamb's paper on *The Old Margate Hoy* who "when we asked him whether he had any friends where he was going," replied, "he *had* no friends." Solitariness is ever the appeal of such a figure; an unbefriendedness that "makes friends," searching straight to our common charity: this and the attraction of youth, knocking—so to speak—on the house-door of our own lost or locked-away ambitions. "Is there anybody there?" says this Traveller, and he, unlike the older one (who is oneself), gets an answer. The mid-Victorian Dr. Smiles saw him as an embryonic Lord Mayor dazed amid the traffic on London Bridge but clutching at his one half-crown for fear of pick-pockets. I myself met him once in a crowded third-class railway carriage. He was fifteen and bound for the sea: and when we came in sight of it he pushed past our knees to the carriage window and broke into a high tuneless chant, all oblivious of us. Challenge was in it and a sob of desire at sight of his predestined mistress and adversary. For the sea is great, but the heart in any given boy may be greater: and

> these things are life
> And life, some think, is worthy of the Muse.

III

But I am a Professor, and ought to have begun by assuring you that this figure in Westminster Hall has a real historical interest in connexion with your studies "on the subject of English Literature."

Well, then, it has. The date of the apparition is New Year's Day, 1834, and by New Year's Day, 1838, Charles Dickens was not only the most popular of living authors, but in a fair way to become that which he remained until the end in 1870—a great National Institution.

I use no exaggerated term. Our fathers of the nineteenth century had a way (and perhaps not altogether a bad way) of considering their great writers as national institutions; Carlyle was one, Ruskin another. It was a part of their stout individualism, nowadays derided. And it was, if you will consider, in the depths of its soul [say, if you will, its Manchester Soul] a high-polite retort upon such a sworn enemy as Ruskin. "Curse us, Sir: but *we* and no *Government* make you a demigod." You will never understand your fathers, Gentlemen, until you understand their proud distrust of Government save by consent. Take a favourite term of theirs—say "The Liberty of the Press." By that *they* meant liberty from interference by *Government*. *We*, using that term to-day, should mean nothing of the sort. *We* should mean "liberty from control by capitalists."

I interrogate my youthful memories and am confident that, in a modest country household these men —Carlyle, Ruskin—were, with decent reverence, though critically, read for prophets. Tennyson, too, and Browning had their sacred niches; and Darwin and Huxley, and Buckle, who perished young attempting a *History of Civilisation in Europe:* John Stuart Mill, also, and Kingsley, Maurice, George Eliot, and Thackeray. These names leap to memory as names of household gods. A few weeks ago, rummaging over some family papers I came upon the following entry:

1848, June 20. I received a visit from Mr. Alfred Tennyson, the Poet. He came into Cornwall along the North Coast, and from about Camelford crossed over to Fowey, where I called on him on the 19th. He came to Polperre in a boat, with Mr. Peach and others; and after viewing our scenery in all directions and taking tea at our house, they all rowed back to Fowey late in the evening. I find him well-informed and communicative. I believe a good Greek scholar with some knowledge of Hebrew. His personal appearance is not prepossessing; having a slouch in his gait and rather slovenly in his dress tho' his clothes were new and good. He confesses to this. He admired the wildness of our scenery, deprecated the breaking in of improvements, as they are termed. He enquired after traditions, especially of the great Arthur: his object in visiting the County being to collect materials for a poem on that Chief. But he almost doubted his existence. He show'd me a MS. sketch of a history of the Hero: but it was prolix and modern.

You see, hinted in this extract from a journal, how our ancestors, in 1848 and the years roundabout, and in remote parts of England, welcomed these great men as gods: albeit critically, being themselves stout fellows. But above all these, from the publication of *Pickwick* —or, to be precise, of its fifth number, in which (as Beatrice would say) "there was a star danced" and under it Sam Weller was born—down to June 14, 1870, and the funeral in Westminster Abbey, Dickens stood exalted, in a rank apart. Nay, when he had been laid in the grave upon which, left and right, face the monuments of Chaucer, Shakespeare and Dryden, and for days after the grave was closed, the stream of unbidden mourners went by. "All day long," wrote Dean Stanley on the 17th, "there was a constant pressure on the spot, and many flowers were strewn on it by unknown hands, many tears shed from unknown eyes."

Without commenting on it for the moment, I want you to realise this exaltation of Dickens in the popular mind, his countrymen's and countrywomen's intimate,

passionate pride in him; in the first place because it is
an historical fact, and a fact (I think) singular in our
literary history; but also because, as a phenomenon
itself unique—unique, at any rate, in its magnitude—it
reacted singularly upon the man and his work, and you
must allow for this if you would thoroughly understand
either.

IV

To begin with, you must get it out of your minds
that it resembled any popularity known to us, in our
day: the deserved popularity of Mr. Kipling, for example. You must also (of this generation I may be asking
a hard thing, but it is necessary) get it out of your
minds that Dickens was, in any sense at all, a cheap
artist playing to the gallery. He was a writer of imperfect, or hazardous, literary education: but he was
also a man of iron will and an artist of the fiercest
literary conscience. Let me enforce this by quoting
two critics whom you will respect. "The faults of
Dickens," says William Ernest Henley,

were many and grave. He wrote some nonsense; he sinned
repeatedly against taste; he could be both noisy and vulgar; he was apt to be a caricaturist where he should have
been a painter; he was often mawkish and often extravagant; and he was sometimes more inept than a
great writer has ever been. But his work, whether good or
bad, has in full measure the quality of sincerity. He
meant what he did; and he meant it with his whole heart.
He looked upon himself as representative and national—
as indeed he was; he regarded his work as a universal
possession; and he determined to do nothing that for lack
of pains should prove unworthy of his function. If he

sinned, it was unadvisedly and unconsciously; if he failed it was because he knew no better. You feel that as you read. . . .

He had enchanted the public without an effort: he was the best beloved of modern writers almost from the outset of his career. But he had in him at least as much of the French artist as of the middle-class Englishman; and if all his life he never ceased from self-education, but went unswervingly in pursuit of culture, it was out of love for his art and because his conscience as an artist would not let him do otherwise.

Now let me add this testimony from Mr. G. K. Chesterton:

Dickens stands first as a defiant monument of what happens when a great literary genius has a literary taste akin to that of the community. For the kinship was deep and spiritual. Dickens was not like our ordinary demagogues and journalists. Dickens did not write what the people wanted. Dickens wanted what the people wanted. . . . Dickens never talked down to the people. He talked up to the people. He approached the people like a deity and poured out his riches and his blood. He had not merely produced something they could understand, but he took it seriously, and toiled and agonised to produce it. They were not only enjoying one of the best writers, they were enjoying the best he could do. His raging and sleepless nights, his wild walks in the darkness, his note-books crowded, his nerves in rags, all this extraordinary output was but a fit sacrifice to the ordinary man.

"The good, the gentle, high-gifted, ever-friendly, noble Dickens," wrote Carlyle of him, on hearing the news of his death,—"every inch of him an honest man." "What a face it is to meet," had said Leigh Hunt, years before; and Mrs. Carlyle, "It was as if made of steel."

V

I shall endeavour to appraise with you, by and by,
the true worth of this amazing popularity. For the
moment I merely ask you to consider the fact and the
further fact that Dickens took it with the seriousness
it deserved and endeavoured more and more to make
himself adequate to it. He had—as how could he help
having?—an enormous consciousness of the power he
wielded: a consciousness which in action too often displayed itself as an irritable conscientiousness. For instance, *Pickwick* is a landmark in our literature: its
originality can no more be disputed than the originality (say) of the *Divina Commedia*. "I thought of
Pickwick"—is his classical phrase. He thought of Pickwick—and Pickwick was. But just because the ill-
fated illustrator, Seymour—who shot himself before
the great novel had found its stride—was acclaimed
by some as its inventor, Dickens must needs charge
into the lists with the hottest, angriest, most super-
fluous, denials. Even so, later on, when he finds it
intolerable to go on living with his wife, the world is,
somehow or other, made acquainted with this distressing domestic affair as though by a papal encyclical.
Or, even so, when he chooses (in *Bleak House*) to
destroy an alcoholised old man by "spontaneous combustion"—quite unnecessarily—a solemn preface has
to be written to explain that such an end is scientifically
possible. This same conscientiousness made him (and
here our young novelist of to-day will start to blas-
pheme) extremely scrupulous about scandalising his
public—I use the term in its literal sense of laying a
stumbling-block, a cause of offence. For example,
while engaged upon *Dombey and Son*, he has an idea

(and a very good idea too, though he abandoned it) that instead of keeping young Walter the unspoilt boyish lover that he is, he will portray the lad as gradually yielding to moral declension, through hope deferred —a theme which, as you will remember, he afterwards handled in *Bleak House:* and he seriously writes thus about it to his friend Forster:

About the boy, who appears in the last chapter of the first number—I think it would be a good thing to disappoint all the expectations that chapter seems to raise of his happy connection with the story and the heroine, and to show him gradually and naturally trailing away, from that love of adventure and boyish light-heartedness, into negligence, idleness, dissipation, dishonesty and ruin. To show, in short, that common, every day, miserable declension of which we know so much in our ordinary life: to exhibit something of the philosophy of it, in great temptations and an easy nature; and to show how the good turns into the bad, by degrees. If I kept some notion of Florence always at the bottom of it, *I think it might be made very powerful and very useful. What do you think? Do you think it may be done without making people angry?*

George Gissing—in a critical study of Dickens which cries out for reprinting—imagines a young writer of the 'nineties (as we may imagine a young writer of to-day) coming on that and crying out upon it.

What! a great writer, with a great idea, to stay his hand until he has made grave enquiry whether Messrs. Mudie's subscribers will approve it or not! The mere suggestion is infuriating. . . . Look at Flaubert, for example. Can you imagine *him* in such a sorry plight? Why, nothing would have pleased him better than to know he was outraging public sentiment! In fact, it is only when one *does* so that one's work has a chance of being good.

All which, adds Gissing, may be true enough in relation to the speaker. As regards Dickens, it is irrelevant. And Gissing speaks the simple truth; "that he owed it to his hundreds of thousands of readers to teach them a new habit of judgment Dickens did not see or begin to see." But that it lay upon him to deal with his public scrupulously he felt in the very marrow of his bones. Let me give you two instances:

When editing *Household Words* he receives from a raw contributor a MS. impossible as sent, in which he detects merit. "I have had a story," he writes to Forster, "to hack and hew into some form this morning, which has taken me four hours of close attention." "Four hours of Dickens' time," comments Gissing, "in the year 1856, devoted to such a matter as this!—where any ordinary editor, or rather his assistant, would have contented himself with a few blottings and insertions, sure that 'the great big stupid heart of the public,' as Thackeray called it, would be no better pleased, toil how one might."

For my second instance. The next year, 1857, was Mutiny Year, and closed upon an England raging mad over the story of Cawnpore. Dickens and Wilkie Collins, on a tour together in the north of England, had contrived a Christmas Number for *Household Words*, announced and entitled *The Perils of Certain English Prisoners, and their Treasures in Women, Children, Silver and Jewels.* The public expected a red-hot account of the Nana Sahib, the treacherous embarkation, the awful voyage down the Ganges. It was all there, to the man's hand, with illimitable

applause for his mere inviting. But it might inflame—
and, inflaming, hurt—the nation's temper, and therefore he would have none of it: he, Dickens, the great
literary Commoner; lord over millions of English and
to them, and to right influence on them, bounden.
Therefore the public got something more profitable
than it craved for: it got a romantic story empty of
racial or propagandist hatred; a simple narrative of
peril and adventure on a river in South America.

VI

But now let us see what a light this conscious popularity throws upon two important events in Dickens'
career: his visit to the United States in 1842, and his
invention, the next year, of the "Christmas Book."

Dickens went over to America as a great personage:
securely, but neither immodestly nor overweeningly
conscious of it. He went over also as a great and
genuine early-Victorian radical; something better than
any politician; an unbribed and unbribable writer,
immensely potent, with a pen already dedicated to war
against social abuses. He landed at Boston, fully ex-
pecting to see Liberty in realisation under the star-
spangled banner. He found Colonel Diver and Mr.
Jefferson Brick, Mr. La Fayette Kettle and the Honourable Elijah Pogram. He found, of course, a fervent
and generous hospitality that sprang, in Forster's
words, "from feelings honourable both to giver and
receiver," and was bestowed sincerely, if with a touch
of bravado and challenge—"We of the New World
want to show you, by extending the kind of homage
that the Old World reserves for kings and conquerors,
to a young man with nothing to distinguish him but his

heart and his genius, what it is we think in these parts worthier of honour than birth or wealth, a title or a sword." These are Forster's words again, and they do well enough. The hospitality included no doubt a good deal of the ridiculous: food for innocent caricature of the kind provided in the great Pogram levee where the two Literary Ladies are presented to the Honourable Elijah by the Mother of the Modern Gracchi.

"To be presented to a Pogram," said Miss Codger, "by a Hominy, indeed a thrilling moment is it in its impressiveness on what we call our feelings. But why we call them so, and why impressed they are, or if impressed they are at all, or if at all we are, or if there really is, oh gasping one! a Pogram or a Hominy, or any active principle to which we give those titles is a topic, Spirit searching, light-abandoned, much too vast to enter on, at this unlooked-for Crisis." "Mind and Matter," said the lady in the wig, "glide swift into the vortex of immensity. Howls the sublime, and softly sleeps the calm Ideal, in the whispering chambers of Imagination. To hear it, sweet it is. But then outlaughs the stern philosopher, and saith to the Grotesque, 'What ho! arrest for me that agency! Go bring it here! And so the vision fadeth.'"

I will not take oath that I have not heard faint echoes of that sort of talk at literary gatherings within a mile or so of this very spot. But if it be not to some extent endemic in America even to-day, then all I can say is that certain American authors (Mrs. Edith Wharton for one) have misrepresented it far more cruelly than ever did Charles Dickens, or certainly than I, with no knowledge at all, have any wish to do.

But what brought Dickens up with a round turn was

his discovery (as he believed) that in this land of freedom no man was free to speak his thought.

"I believe," he wrote to Forster on Feb. 24th, "there is no country on the face of the earth where there is less freedom of opinion on any subject in reference to which there is a broad difference of opinion than in this. . . . There!—I write the words with reluctance, disappointment and sorrow: but I believe it from the bottom of my soul."

He did believe it, and it shocked him inexpressibly. "Very well," it may be answered; "but there were obligations. A man should not publicly criticise a country in which he is an honoured guest." Yes, but he had gone out to the States with intent to discuss the question of copyright, or rather of literary piracy, in which American law and practice were so flagrantly immoral that he had never a doubt of getting both rectified by a little heart-to-heart talk (as we call it now) with some of their public men and lawgivers. Dickens was always a good man of business. As the most widely-read of British authors, and therefore the chief of sufferers, he could speak authoritatively on behalf of his poorer brethren. He went, and received on a grand scale that shock which on a far modester scale many of us have experienced in our time, with the sort of embarrassment one feels (let us say) in sitting down to Bridge with a very delightful person whose code in the matter of revoking is rather notoriously "off colour." Let me illustrate this by the remark of a just man at Washington in the debate preceding the latest copyright enactment. A member of Congress had pleaded for the children of the back-woods—these potential Abraham Lincolns devouring education by the light of pine-knot fires—how desirable that these little Sons of Liberty should be able to purchase their books (as he put it) "free of authorial expenses!" "Hear, hear!" retorted my just man. "And the negroes of the South too—so fond of chicken free of *farmer-ial* expenses!"—A great saying!

And yet Dickens was wrong: in my opinion wrong as an English Gentleman, being America's Guest. On the balance I hold that he should have thought what he thought and, thinking it, have shortened his visit and come silently away.

Well, Dickens discussed the matter with Washington Irving, Prescott, Hoffman, Bryant, Dana and others, and found that while every writer in America was agreed upon the atrocious state of the law, not a man of them dared to speak out. The suggestion that an American could be found with temerity enough to hint that his country was possibly wrong struck the boldest dumb. "Then," said Dickens, "I shall speak out": and he did. "I wish you could have seen," he writes home, "the faces that I saw, down both sides of the table at Hartford, when I began to talk about Scott." [Remember, please, this is my interjection, Gentlemen, that, on a small portion of his dues, on a 10 per cent. (say) of his plundered sales, the great Sir Walter Scott would have died in calm of mind and just prosperity.] "I wish you could have heard how I gave it out. My blood so boiled as I thought of the monstrous injustice that I felt as if I were twelve feet high when I thrust it down their throats."

The violence of the reaction upon Dickens you can of course study in *American Notes* and *Martin Chuzzlewit*. But the real import of these two books and the violence of resentment they raised, we shall not understand without realising that Dickens went over, was feasted: was disappointed, then outraged, and spoke his mind, from first to last *as a representative of the democracy of this country*, always conscious of a great, if undefined, responsibility and, under disappointment, resolute to be brave, at whatever cost of favour.

VII

The same grand consciousness seems to me to have been the true inspiration of his "Christmas Books." For a private confession, I dislike them: I find them—*A Christmas Carol, The Chimes, The Cricket on the Hearth, The Battle of Life, The Haunted Man*—grossly sentimental and as grossly overcharged with violent conversions to the "Christmas Spirit." For a further confession I greatly prefer several of his later Christmas Stories in *Household Words* and *All the Year Round*— *The Wreck of the "Golden Mary"* for instance, or *Dr. Marigold's Prescriptions* or *The Holly-Tree Inn*—to this classic five which are still separated in the collected editions under the title of "Christmas Books." He himself confessed, in a general preface of less than a dozen lines, his inability to work out character in the limits he assigned himself—a hundred pages or so. "My chief purpose," he says of *A Christmas Carol*, "was, in a whimsical kind of masque which the good humour of the season justified, to awaken some loving and forbearing thoughts, never out of season in a Christian land." But he took it as a mission, and quite seriously. Christmas to England had always meant, and should mean, a festival of neighbourly goodwill and robust hospitality. Listen to the old Carols:

Now thrice welcome, Christmas,
  Which brings us good cheer,
Minced pies and plum porridge,
  Good ale and strong beer;
With pig, goose and capon,
  The best that may be,
So well doth the weather
  And our stomachs agree.

Or

Now that the time is come wherein
  Our Saviour Christ was born,
The larders full of beef and pork,
  The garners fill'd with corn. . . .

Or

Bring us in good ale, and bring us in good ale;
For our blessed Lady's sake, bring us in good ale.

These out of a score or more verses I might quote from
Poor Robin's Almanack and the like. But take Campion's more aristocratic Muse:

Now winter nights enlarge
  The number of their hours,
And clouds their storms discharge
  Upon the airy towers.
Let now the chimneys blaze
  And cups o'erflow with wine;
Let well-attuned words amaze
  With harmony divine.
  Now yellow waxen lights
  Shall wait on honey love,
While youthful revels, masques, and courtly sights
  Sleep's leaden spell remove.

Carry this again down to Frederick Tennyson's *The Holy Tide:*

The days are sad, it is the Holy tide;
  The Winter morn is short, the Night is long;
So let the lifeless Hours be glorified
  With deathless thoughts and echo'd in sweet song:
And through the sunset of this purple cup
  They will resume the roses of their prime,
And the old Dead will hear us and wake up,
  Pass with dim smiles and make our hearts sublime.

"An Englishman's house is his Castle," said an immortal farmer at a Fat Stock Dinner. "The storms may assail it and the winds whistle round it, but the King himself cannot do so." Dickens saw always the Englishman's house as his castle, fortified and provisioned against the discharge of snow and sleet: always most amply provisioned! Witness his picture of Christmas at Manor Farm, Dingley Dell—Old Wardle with his friends, neighbours, poor relations, and his farm-labourers too, all sitting down together to a colossal supper "and a mighty bowl of wassail something smaller than an ordinary washhouse copper, in which the hot apples were hissing and bubbling with a rich look and jolly sound that were perfectly irresistible."

Old Wardle, in fact, is in the direct line of succession to Chaucer's Frankeleyne—

> Withoute bake mete was never his hous,
> Of fish and flesh, and that so plenteous,
> It snewed in his hous of mete and drink.

Dickens, I repeat to you, was always, in the straight line of Chaucer, Ben Jonson, Dryden, Fielding, a preacher of man's dignity in his full appetite; and quite consciously, as a national genius, he preached the doctrine of Christmas to his nation.

VIII

But you will say perhaps "Granted his amazing popularity—granted, too, his right to assume on it— was it really deserved?" To this question I oppose for the moment my opinion that, were I asked to choose out of the story of English Literature a short list of the most fecund authors, I should start with Chaucer, Marlowe, Shakespeare, Donne, Dryden, Pope, Samuel Johnson, Burke, Gibbon, Wordsworth, Coleridge, Shelley, Keats, Carlyle, Dickens, Browning. If compelled to reduce the list to three, choosing the three most lavishly endowed by God with imagination for their fellows' good, I almost think that among all God's plenty I should choose, as pre-eminent stars, Shakespeare, Burke and Dickens. Milton, of course, will stand apart always, a solitary star: and Chaucer for his amazing invention, less even for what he did than for that he did it at all; Keats for infinity of promise; and to exclude Scott seems almost an outrage on human kindness. Yet if it come to the mere wonder-work of genius—the creation of men and women, on a page of paper, who are actually more real to us than our daily acquaintances, as companionable in a crowd as even our best selected friends, as individual as the most eccentric we know, yet as universal as humanity itself, I do not see what English writer we can choose to put second to Shakespeare save Charles Dickens. I am talking of sheer creative power, as I am thinking of Tasso's proud saying that, next to God himself, no one but the poet deserves the name of Creator. You feel of Dickens as of Shakespeare that anything may happen: because it is not with them as with other authors: it is not they who speak. Falstaff or Hamlet or Sam Weller or Mr. Micawber: it is the god speaking:

Ἄνδρα μοι ἔννεπε, Μοῦσα.

They are as harps upon which the large wind plays: and as that is illimitable there is no limit to their utterances. It was so with Charles Dickens from the Sam Weller of his lost youth down to the last when, in pain and under the shadow of death, he invented the Billickin.

In another lecture I propose to show you (if I can) that Dickens' characters belong to a world of his own, rather than to this one. But if he also created that world of his own, so much the grander creator he!—As if he made men and women walk and talk in it, compelling us to walk with them, and listen, and, above all, open our lungs and laugh, suffer within the tremendous illusion, so much is he the more potent magician! I also feel, in reading Shakespeare, or Dickens—I would add Burke—as I feel with no fourth that I am dealing with a scope of genius quite incalculable; that while it keeps me proud to belong to their race and nation and to inherit their speech, it equally keeps me diffident because, at any turn of the page may occur some plenary surprise altogether beyond my power or scope of guessing. With these three writers, as with no fourth, *I* have the sensation of a certain *faintness* of enjoyment, of surrender, to be borne along as on vast wings. Yet of Dickens, as of Shakespeare, the worst work can be incredibly bad. Sorrier stuff could scarcely be written, could scarcely conceivably have ever been written, than the whole part of Speed in *The Two Gentlemen of Verona* unless it be the first chapter of *Martin Chuzzlewit*. Yet in *Martin Chuzzlewit* you get Mrs. Gamp: and I ask you, How much the poorer should we not all be, lacking Mrs. Gamp?

I grant you that he has not yet passed—as he has not yet had time to pass—the *great* test of a classical writer; which is that, surviving the day's popularity and its conditions, his work goes on meaning more, under quite different conditions, to succeeding ages; the great test which Shakespeare has passed more than once or twice, remaining to-day, though quite differently, even more significant than he was to his contemporaries. I grant —as in another lecture I shall be at pains to show— that Dickens' plots were usually incredible, often monstrous. But he invented a world: he peopled it with men and women for our joy: and my confidence in the diuturnity of his fame rests even on more than this—on the experience that, test this genius by whatever standard a critic may, he has by and by to throw down his measure and admit that, while Dickens was always a learner, out of his prodigality he could have at any moment knocked the critic over by creating a new world with new and delectable lasting characters to take it in charge.

DICKENS (II)

I

I TAKE up my parable for a few words more upon the point at which I broke off last week—the essential *greatness* of Dickens. For greatness is a quality in some few men: indefinable perhaps, but yet to be recognised; a certain thing and, by those of us who would traffic with life or literature, not to be overlooked or denied save at our soul's peril, no matter what standard of artistry or of refined scholarship we may set up: a *quality* in itself, moreover, and not any addition or multiplication or raising of talent by industry. For an illustration of the peril: I was reading, the other day, a history of French Literature by the late M. Ferdinand Brunetière, and, coming to the time of Alexandre Dumas the elder, I found that the historian, disapproving of Dumas, has just left him out! Now that, I contend (saving M. Brunetière's eminence), is to write oneself down a pedant, outside the catholic mind. Dumas lived a scandalous life, wrote much execrable French, and encouraged—even employed—some of his fellows to write worse. But the author of *The Three Musketeers*, *Le Vicomte de Bragelonne*, *La Reine Margot* —Dumas, "the seven-and-seventy times to be forgiven," is not to be treated so, by your leave: or only so, I repeat, at the critic's peril. Or let me take an Englishman—John Dryden. I suspect I shall not

misrepresent or misreport the attitude of many in this
room towards Dryden when I say that we find a world
of slovenly sorry stuff in his dramas, and in his poems
a deal of wit and rhetoric which our later taste—such as
it is, good or bad, true or false—refuses to pass for
poetry at all.   Now if I merely wanted to prove to you
that Dryden at his best could write finely, exquisitely—
that out of the strong could come forth sweetness—I
could content myself with asking you to listen to these
verses:

> No, no, poor suffering heart, no change endeavour,
> Choose to sustain the smart, rather than leave her;
> My ravish'd eyes behold such charms about her,
> I can die with her, but not live without her·
> One tender sigh of her, to see me languish,
> Will more than pay the price of my past anguish;
> Beware, O cruel fair, how you smile on me,
> 'Twas a kind look of yours that has undone me.
>
> *Love* has in store for me one happy minute,
> And she will end my pain, who did begin it;
> Then no day, void of bliss, of pleasure, leaving,
> Ages shall slide away without perceiving:
> *Cupid* shall guard the door, the more to please us,
> And keep out *Time* and *Death*, when they would seize us:
> *Time* and *Death* shall depart, and say in flying,
> "Love has found out a way to live—by dying."

There, obviously, is a *virtuoso* who commands his key-
board.   But if I were talking about Dryden to you for
your soul's good, I should rather show you the man
with all his imperfections on his head, then turn and
challenge you to deny his greatness.   Why, you can
scarcely read a page, even of his prose—say, for choice,

the opening of his *Essay of Dramatic Poesy*—without recognising the tall fellow of his hands, the giant among his peers,

$$\psi\upsilon\chi\grave{\eta}\ldots$$
$$\ldots\mu\alpha\kappa\rho\grave{\alpha}\ \beta\iota\beta\tilde{\alpha}\sigma\alpha\ \kappa\alpha\tau'\ \dot{\alpha}\sigma\phi o\delta\epsilon\lambda\grave{o}\nu\ \lambda\epsilon\iota\mu\tilde{\omega}\nu\alpha,$$

"pacing with long stride the asphodel meadow" where, let us say, Samuel Johnson walks, and Handel, and Hugo, nor are they abashed to salute the very greatest —Dante, Michelangelo, Shakespeare.

I repeat, Gentlemen, that at all risk of appearing exorbitant I should preach this to you for your souls' good. For I do most earnestly want you, before all else, to recognise this *quality* of greatness and respond to it. In so far as, in your fleeting generation, you give me your confidence and honour me (shall I say?) with a personal hope for A or B or C, I would warn you of what I have experimentally proved to be true of my contemporaries—that the man is most fatally destined to be great himself who learns early to enlarge his heart to the great masters; that those have steadily sunk who cavilled at Caesar with Cassius, or over a cigarette chatted admiringly of the rent which envious Casca made: that anyone with an ear learns very surely to distinguish the murmur of the true bee from the morose hum of the drone who is bringing no honey, nor ever will, to the hive. In my own time of apprenticeship —say in the 'nineties—we were all occupied—after the French novelists—with style: in seeking the right word, *le mot juste*, and with "art for art's sake," etc. And we were serious enough, mind you. We cut ourselves with knives. To-day, if I may diagnose your more youthful sickness, you are occupied rather with lyricism,

curious and recondite sensations, appositions of un-
related facts with magenta-coloured adjectives. The
craze has spread to the shop-fronts, to curtains, bed-
spreads, as the craze for Byronic collars spread in its
day: and "Hell is empty!" cried Ferdinand, plunging
overboard: but you can still find psycho-analysis
rampant, with any amount of Birth Control, among
the geese on Golder's Green. But if from this desk I
have preached incessantly on a text, it is this—that all
spirit being mutually attractive, as all matter is mutually attractive, is an ultimate fact: and that therefore
we shall grow the greater and better critics as we surrender ourselves to the great writers and without
detraction, at least until we have, in modesty of mind,
proved them: since, to apply a word of Emerson's:

> Heartily know—
> When half-gods go,
> The gods arrive.

II

So I broke off, or almost, upon a saying of Tasso's—
you may find it repeated in Ben Jonson's *Timber, or
Discoveries*—that in this world none deserves the name
of Creator save God himself and the Poet—by "Poet"
meaning, of course, the great imaginative artist whether
working in restricted verse or in "that other harmony
of prose."

And you may be thinking—I don't doubt, a number
will be thinking—that in a discourse on Dickens, I am
putting the claim altogether too high. I can feel your
minds working, I think—working to some such tune
as this "Dickens and Virgil, now—Dickens and Dante
—Oh, heaven alive!'"

You cannot say that I have shirked it—can you?

Well now, fair and softly! If I had said "Dickens and Shakespeare," it would have given you no such shock: and if I had said "Shakespeare and Dante," or "Dickens and Molière," it would have given you no shock at all. I am insisting, you understand, that the first test of greatness in an imaginative writer is his power to create: and I propose to begin with that which, if there should by any chance happen to be a fool in this apparently representative gathering, he will infallibly despise for the easiest thing in the world, the creation of a fool. I beg to reassure him and, so far as I can, restore his self-respect. It is about the hardest thing in the world, to create a fool and laugh at him. It is a human, nay, even a Godlike function (so and not by others shared) to laugh. Listen, before we go further, to these stanzas on divine laughter:

Nay, 'tis a Godlike function; laugh thy fill!
Mirth comes to thee unsought:
Mirth sweeps before it like a flood the mill
Of languaged logic: thought
Hath not its source so high;
The will
Must let it by:
For, though the heavens are still,
God sits upon His hill
And sees the shadows fly:
And if He laughs at fools, why should He not?
"Yet hath the fool a laugh"—Yea, of a sort;
God careth for the fools;
The chemic tools
Of laughter He hath given them, and some **toys**
Of sense, as 'twere a small retort
Wherein they may collect the joys

Of natural giggling, as becomes their state:
The fool is not inhuman, making sport
For such as would not gladly be without
That old familiar noise:
Since, though he laugh not, he can cachinnate—
This also is of God, we may not doubt.

Shakespeare, as we know, delighted in a fool, and
revelled in creating one. (I need hardly say that I am
not talking of the professionals, such as Touchstone or
the Fool in *Lear*, who are astute critics rather, ridiculing
the folly of their betters by reflexion by some odd facet
of common sense, administering hellebore to minds
diseased and so in their function often reminding us
of the Chorus in Greek tragedy.) I mean, of course, the
fool in his *quiddity*, such as Dogberry, or Mr. Justice
Shallow, or Cousin Abraham Slender. Hearken to
Dogberry:

Dog. Come hither, neighbour Seacole. God hath blessed
you with a good name: to be a well-favoured man is the
gift of fortune; but to write and read comes by nature.
Sec. Watch. Both which, master Constable—
Dog. You have: I knew it would be your answer.
Well, for your favour, sir, why, give God thanks, and
make no boast of it; and for your writing and reading,
let that appear when there is no need of such vanity.

Why, it might be an extract from the Geddes Report
—or so much of it as deals with Education!
And now to Slender, bidden in by sweet Anne Page
to her father's dinner-table:

Anne. Will it please your worship to come in, sir?
Slender. No—I thank you, forsooth—heartily. I am
very well.

Anne. The dinner attends you, sir.

Slender. I am not a-hungry, I thank you, forsooth. . . .

Anne. I may not go in without your worship; they will not sit till you come.

Slender. I'faith, I'll eat nothing: I thank you as much as though I did.

Anne. I pray you, sir, walk in.

Slender. I had rather walk here—I thank you. I bruised my shin th' other day with playing at sword and dagger with a master of fence—three veneys for a dish of stewed prunes—and, I with my ward defending my head, he shot my shin, and by my troth, I cannot abide the smell of hot meat since. . . . Why do your dogs bark so? Be there bears in town?

Anne. I think there are, sir. I heard them talked of.

Slender. I love the sport well, but I shall as soon quarrel at it as any man in England. . . . *You* are afraid, if you see a bear loose, are you not?

Anne. Ay, indeed, sir.

Slender. That's meat and drink to me, now: I have seen Sackerson loose—twenty times, and have taken him by the chain. . . . But women, indeed, cannot abide 'em— they *are* very ill-favoured rough things.

"Othello," as Hartley Coleridge noted, "could not brag more amorously": and, as I wrote the other day in an introduction to *The Merry Wives*, when Anne finally persuades him to walk before her into the house, my fellow-editor and I had written (but afterwards in cowardice erased) the stage-direction, *He goes in: she follows with her apron spread, as if driving a goose.* Yes, truly, Slender is a goose to say grace over and to be carved "as a dish fit for the gods." "A very potent piece of imbecility," writes Hazlitt, and adds, "Shakespeare is the only writer who was as great in describing weakness as strength."

Well, Jane Austen and Charles Dickens came after,
to confirm Hazlitt's observation. No one seeks in
Jane Austen for examples of strength: and you will
find none in Dickens to compare with Othello or
Cleopatra or (say) with Mr. Hardy's Mayor of Caster-
bridge. But, like Charles Lamb, Jane Austen and
Dickens both "loved a fool": Jane Austen delicately,
Dickens riotously: witness the one's Miss Bates, the
other's Mr. Toots. But observe, pray: the fools they
delight in are always—like Slender, like Miss Bates,
like Mr. Toots—simple fools, sincere fools, good at
heart, good to live with, and in their way, the salt of
the earth. Miss Bates herself bears unconscious
witness to this in one of her wisest foolishest remarks—
"It is such a happiness when good people get together—
and they always do." (Consoling thought for you and
me at this very moment.) With the fool who is also
a humbug, a self-deceiver, Dickens could find no
patience in his heart; and this impatience of his you
may test again and again, always to find it—if I may
say so with reverence—as elementary as our Lord's.
I am not speaking of conscious, malignant hypocrites—
your Stiggins's, Pecksniffs, Chadbands—on whom
Dickens waged war, his life through; but of the self-
deceiving fool whom we will agree with him in calling
an "ass"—Uncle Pumblechook, for instance, in *Great
Expectations*, Mr. Sapsea in *Edwin Drood*; on whom,
or on whose kind, as he grew older, he seems (most of
all in his last book, whenever handling Mr. Sapsea) to
lose his artistic self-control, to savage them. But of
kind fools, lovable fools, good fools, God's fools,
Dickens' heaven will open any moment at call and
rain you down half-a-dozen, all human, each distinct.
You may count half-a-dozen in his most undeservedly

misprised book, *Little Dorrit*, omitting Mr. F.'s Aunt:
who is an eccentric, rather, though an unforgettable one
and has left her unforgettable mark on the world in less
than 200 words. She stands apart: for the others,
apart from foolishness, share but one gift in common,
a consanguinity (as it were) in flow of language or
determination of words to the mouth. Shall we select
the vulgar, breathless, good-natured widow, Flora
Finching, ever recalling the past (without so much
pause as a comma's) to her disillusioned first lover?—

In times for ever fled Arthur pray excuse me Doyce and
Clennam (the name of his firm) infinitely more correct and
though unquestionably distant still 'tis distance lends en-
chantment to the view, at least I don't mean that and if I
did I suppose it would depend considerably on the nature
of the view, but I'm running on again and you put it all
out of my head.

She glanced at him tenderly and resumed:

In times for ever fled I was going to say it would have
sounded strange indeed for Arthur Clennam—Doyce and
Clennam naturally quite different—to make apologies for
coming here at any time, but that is past and what is past
can never be recalled except in his own case as poor Mr. F.
said when in spirits Cucumber and therefore never ate it.
. . . Papa is sitting prosingly, breaking his new laid
egg over the City article, exactly like the Woodpecker
Tapping, and need never know that you are here. . . .

The withered chaplet is then perished the column is
crumbled and the pyramid is standing upside down upon
its what's-his-name call it not giddiness call it not weakness call it not folly I must now retire into privacy and
looking upon the ashes of departed joys no more but taking the further liberty of paying for the pastry which
has formed the humble pretext for our interview, will for
ever say Adieu!

Mr. F.'s Aunt who had eaten her pie with great solemnity . . . and who had been elaborating some griev-
ous scheme of injury in her mind, took the present opportunity of addressing the following sibyllic apostrophe to
the relict of her late nephew: "Bring him for'ard, and I'll
chuck him out o' winder!"

III

Mr. Chesterton, selecting another fool from the
gallery—Young Mr. Guppy, of *Bleak House*—observes
very wisely, that we may disapprove of Mr. Guppy, but
we recognise him as a creation flung down like a miracle
out of an upper sphere: we can pull him to pieces, but
we could not have put him together. And this (says
he) is the pessimists' disadvantage in criticising any
creation. Even in their attacks on the Universe they
are always under this depressing disadvantage.

"A man looking at a hippopotamus may sometimes
be tempted to regard the hippopotamus as an enormous
mistake: but he is also bound to confess that a fortunate
inferiority prevents him personally from making such
a mistake."

Well, that is, of course, our difficulty in criticising all
creative genius. We tell ourselves how we could have
suggested to Shakespeare—or to Dickens—his doing
this or that better than he did; but the mischief is, *we*
could not have done it at all. And in this matter of
Mr. Guppy, Mr. Chesterton continues: "Not one of us
could have invented Mr. Guppy. But even if we could
have stolen Mr. Guppy from Dickens, we have still to
confront the fact that Dickens would have been able to
invent another quite inconceivable character to take his
place."

IV

Here we get to it. I have instanced his fools only, and but a select two or three of these for a test: but you may take, if you will, shrewd men, miserly men, ruffians, doctors, proctors, prisoners, schoolmasters, coachmen, licensed victuallers, teetotallers, thieves, monthly nurses—whatever the choice be, Dickens will shake them out of his sleeve to populate a world for us. For, like Balzac, he has a world of his own and can at call dispense to us of its abundance.

What sort of a world is it out of which Dickens so enriches ours?

Well, to begin with, it is a crowded world, a world that in his imagination positively teems with folk going, coming, hurrying: of innumerable streets where you may knock in (and welcome) at any chance door to find the house in accumulated misery, poverty, woe, or else in a disorder of sausages and squalling children, with a henpecked husband at one end of the table, a bowl of punch in the middle, and at the other end a mortuary woman whose bus ness in life is to make a burden of life to all who live near her and would have her cheerful. (There was never such a man as Dickens for depicting the blight induced by one ill-tempered person—usually a woman—upon a convivial gathering.) The henpecked husband dispensing the punch is, likely as not, a city clerk contriving a double debt to pay, a slave during office hours, bound to a usurious master: a sort of fairy—a Puck, a Mr. Wemmick, as soon as he sheds his office-coat and makes for somewhere in the uncertain gaslight of the suburbs, "following darkness like a dream."

Yes, this world is of the streets; in which Dickens

was bred and from which he drew the miseries and
consolations of his boyhood.   A world "full of folk,"
but not, like Piers Plowman's, a "*field* full of folk."
His understanding of England is in many ways as deep
as Shakespeare's; but it is all, or almost all, of the urban
England which in his day had already begun to kill the
rural.   I ask you to consider any average drawing of
Phiz's; the number of figures crowded into a little room,
the many absurd things all happening at once, and you
will understand why Phiz was Dickens' favourite illustrator.   A crowded world: an urban world, largely a
middle-class and lower-class London world—what else
could we expect as outcome of a boyhood spent in
poverty and in London?   Of London his knowledge is
indeed, like Sam Weller's, "extensive and peculiar":
with a background or distance of the lower Thames,
black wharves peopled by waterside loafers or sinister
fishers in tides they watch for horrible traffic; rotting
piles such as caught and held the corpse of Quilp.
Some sentiment, indeed, up Twickenham-way: a
handful of flowers, taken from the breast and dropped
at the river's brink, to be floated down, pale and unreal, in the moonlight; "and thus do greater things
that once were in our breasts and near our hearts, flow
from us to the eternal seas."   But before they reach
the eternal seas they must pass Westminster Bridge
whence an inspired dalesman saw the City wearing
the beauty of dawn as a garment.

Ships, towers, domes, theatres and temples . . .
and Waterloo Bridge, Hood's dark arch of tragedy;
and London Bridge, hymned of old by Dunbar.   Dickens' bridge is the old Iron one by Hungerford, and under
it the Thames runs down to ghastly flats, convict-
haunted, below Woolwich.

Shakespeare knew his London, his Eastcheap, its taverns. But when you think of Shakespeare you think (I will challenge you) rather of rural England, of Avon, of Arden, of native wood-notes wild. I hold it doubtful that Falstaff on his death-bed babbled o' green fields: but I will take oath that when he got down to Gloucestershire he smelt the air like a colt or a boy out of school. And Justice Shallow is there—always there!

Silence. This Sir John, cousin, that comes hither anon about soldiers?
Shallow. The same Sir John, the very same. I saw him break Skogan's head at the court-gate, when a' was a crack not *thus* high: and the very same day did I fight with one Sampson Stockfish, a fruiterer, behind Gray's Inn. Jesu, Jesu, the mad days I have spent! and to see how many of my old acquaintance are dead!
Silence. We shall all follow, cousin.
Shallow. Certain, 'tis certain; very sure, very sure: death, as the Psalmist saith, is certain to all; all shall die. How a good yoke of bullocks at Stamford fair?
Silence. By my troth, I was not there.
Shallow. Death is certain. Is old Double of your town living yet?
Silence. Dead, sir.
Shallow. Jesu, Jesu, dead! a' drew a good bow: and dead! a' shot a fine shoot: John a Gaunt loved him well, and betted much money on his head. Dead!—a' would have clapped i' the clout at twelve score; and carried you a forehand shaft a fourteen and fourteen and a half, that it would have done a man's heart good to see. How a score of ewes now?
Silence. Thereafter as they be: a score of good ewes may be worth ten pounds.
Shallow. And is old Double dead?

You get little or none of that solemn, sweet rusticity in Dickens: nor of the rush of England in spring with slow country-folk watching it:

> The fields breathe sweet, the daisies kiss our feet,
> Young lovers meet, old wives a-sunning sit;
> In every street these tunes our ears do greet—
> *Cuckoo, jug-jug, pu-we, to-witta-woo!*
> Spring, the sweet Spring!

You will remember that *Pickwick*, in its first conception, was to deal with the adventures and misadventures of a Sporting Club after the fashion of the *Handley Cross* series by Surtees. Now Surtees—not a great writer but to this day (at any rate to me) a most amusing one—was, although like Dickens condemned to London and the law, a north-country sportsman, and could ride and, it is reported, "without riding for effect usually saw a deal of what the hounds were doing." The Pickwickian sportsmen had to decline *that* competition very soon.

V

But they, and a host of Dickens' characters, are very devils for post-chaises.

"If I had no duties, and no deference to futurity, I would spend my life in driving briskly in a post-chaise with a pretty woman," said Dr. Johnson. "There are milestones on the Dover Road," and we spin past them. You will remember that Dickens in his apprenticeship spent a brief but amazingly strenuous while as reporter for the *Morning Chronicle*, scouring the country after political meetings by road-vehicles in all weathers.   As he told his audience, twenty years later, at the annual dinner of the Newspaper Press Fund:

I have often transcribed for the printer, from my short-hand notes, important public speeches in which the strictest accuracy was required, and a mistake in which would have been, to a young man, severely compromising, writing on the palm of my hand, by the light of a dark lantern, in a post-chaise and four galloping through a wild country, and through the dead of night, at the then surprising rate of fifteen miles an hour. . . . Returning home from exciting political meetings in the country (and it might be from Exeter west, or Manchester north) to the waiting press in London, I do verily believe I have been upset in almost every description of vehicle known in this country.   I have been, in my time, belated in miry by-roads, forty or fifty miles from London, in a wheel-less carriage, with exhausted horses and drunken post-boys, and have got back in time for publication. . . .

So, you see, this world Dickens imagined was more than crowded; it was a hurrying, a breathless one. This sense of speed in travel, of the wind in one's face; of weight and impetus in darkness, with coach lamps flaring through the steam from your good horses' hindquarters, runs as an inspiration through much of the literature of the early nineteenth century.   De Quincey has hymned it magnificently in *The English Mail Coach*, and you may enjoy a capital drive of the sort in *Tom Brown's School Days:* and always the rush of air whets your appetite for the hot rum-and-water at the stage hostelry or the breakfast of kidney-pie.   Dickens saw the invasion of the railway train, and lived to be disastrously mixed up in a railway collision. But railway-train travelling at sixty miles an hour or over, has a static convenience. For the pleasures of inconvenient travel, without a time-table, I have recourse to a sailing-boat: but I can well understand my fellow-creature who prefers a car or a motor-bicycle to the motion of four horses at a stretch gallop. With the wind of God in his face he gets there (wherever it is) before the dew is dry, does his business, swallows his bun and Bovril and is home again with an evening paper for the cosy gas-cooked meal, ere yet Eve has drawn over his little place in the country her gradual dusky veil.

Rapid travel, as Dickens well knew it and how to describe it—with crime straining from what it fears— is one of his most potent resources. Read the flight of Carker in *Dombey and Son*.

VI

His is a crowded world then, tumultuous and full of fierce hurry: but a world (let us grant it) strangely empty of questioning ideas, subtle nuisances that haunt many thoughtful men's souls, through this pass of existence "still clutching the inviolable shade." He wrote far better novels than *John Inglesant*, novels far, far, better than *Robert Ellesmere*; but you cannot con-ceive him as interested in the matter of these books —which yet is serious matter. Still less, or at least as little, can you imagine him pursuing the track of so perplexed a spirit as Prince André in Tolstoy's *War and Peace*. Churches annoyed him. He will, of a christen-ing or a marriage service (let be a funeral), make the mouldiest ceremony in the world. We offer the baby up; we give the blushing bride away; but in the very act we catch ourselves longing for that subsequent chat with the pew-opener which he seldom denies us for reward. Dickens, in short, had little use for religious forms or religious mysteries: for he carried his own religion about with him and it was the religion of James —so annoying alike to the mystic and the formalist— "to visit the fatherless and widows in their affliction, and to keep himself unspotted from the world." This again belongs to his "universality." Is it not the religion of most good fellows not vocal? It is observable how many of his heroes and heroines—his child heroes and heroines especially—pass through his thronged streets and keep themselves unspotted.

But, if careless of mysteries, Dickens had a hawk's eye for truth of morals. You never find him mocking a good or condoning an evil thing: here his judgment and its resultant passion of love or of hate, I dare to say, never went wrong. Sinners—real sinners—in Dickens have the very *inferno* of a time: the very forces of Nature—"fire and hail, snow and vapours, wind and storm, fulfilling God's word"—hunt the murderer to the pit that yawns; till he perishes, and the sky is clear again over holy and humble men of heart. Again, witness, here, the elemental flight of Jonas Chuzzlewit. Carlyle never said an unjuster thing (and that is saying a deal) than when he accused Dickens' theory of life as entirely wrong. "He thought men ought to be buttered up . . . and all sorts of fellows have turkey for their Christmas dinner." It is false. Dickens had a keener eye for sin than Carlyle ever had; and a relentless eye: "a military eye," said Henry James of it, recalling his first introduction to the great man—"a *merciless* military eye." "A field-punishment eye," *I* say!

VII

But this world of Dickens, you may object, was an unreal world, a phantasmagoric world. Well, I hope to discuss that—or rather the inference from it—in my next lecture, which shall deal, in Aristotelian order, with his plots first and his characters next. But, for the moment, if you will, Yes: his world was like nothing on earth: yes, it is liker to Turner's sunset to which the critic objected "he never saw a sunset like that," and was answered, "Ah, but don't you wish you could?" Yes, for Dickens made his world—as the proud parent said of his son's fiddle—"he made it, sir, entirely out of his own head!"

"Night is generally my time for walking" (thus begins Master Humphrey, in *The Old Curiosity Shop*) "although I am an old man."

So in that crowded phantasmagoric city of London, which is in his mind, Dickens walks by night—not like Asmodeus, lifting the roofs and peering into scandals: but like the good Caliph of his favourite *Arabian Nights*, intent to learn the life of the poor and oppressed, and as a monarch to see justice done them: a man patterning his work on the great lines of Fulke Greville, sometime of Jesus College, in this town; with which let me conclude to-day:

> The chief use, then, in man, of that he knows,
> Is his painstaking for the good of all:
> Not fleshly weeping for our own-made woes,
> Not laughing from a melancholy gall,
> Not hating from a soul that overflows
>   With bitterness, breath'd out from inward thrall:
>   But sweetly rather to ease, loose, or bind,
>   As need requires, this frail, fall'n humankind.

DICKENS (III)

I

I LEFT you, Gentlemen, with a promise to say something on Dickens' plots and Dickens' characters, taking them in that Aristotelian order. Now why Aristotle, speaking of drama, prefers Plot to Character; if his reasons are sound; if they are all the reasons; and, anyhow, if they can be transferred from drama and applied to the Novel; are questions which some of you have debated with me "in another place," and, if without heat, yet with all the vigour demanded by so idle a topic. But, for certain, few of you will dissent when I say of Dickens that he is memorable and to be loved (if loved at all) for his characters rather than for his plots. You have (say) a general idea of *Dombey and Son*, a vivid recollection of Captain Cuttle, Mr. Toots, Susan Nipper, perhaps a vivid recollection of Carker's long, hunted flight and its appalling end, when the pursuer, recovering from a swoon—

saw them bringing from a distance something covered . . . upon a board, between four men, and saw that others drove some dogs away that sniffed upon the road, and soaked his blood up, with a train of ashes.

Or you have a general idea of *Our Mutual Friend*, and your memory preserves quite a sharp impression of

Silas Wegg, Mr. Boffin, the Doll's Dressmaker. But if suddenly asked how Carker's flight came about, why Boffin practised his long dissimulation, and what precisely Wegg or the Doll's Dressmaker had to do with it—could you, off-hand, supply a clear answer? Some votaries can, no doubt: but I ask it of the ordinary reader. Myself indeed may claim to be something of a votary, with an inexplicably soft spot in my heart for *Little Dorrit*: yet, and often as I have read that tale, I should be gravelled if asked, at this moment, to tell you just what was the secret of the old house, or just what Miss Wade and Tattycoram have to do with the story. Somehow, in retrospect, such questions do not seem to matter.

In truth, as I see it—and foresee it as a paradox, to be defended—Dickens was at once, like Shakespeare in the main, careless of his plots, and, unlike Shakespeare, over-anxious about them. I shall stress this second point, which stabs (I think) to the truth beneath the paradox, by and by.

But first I ask you to remember that Dickens habitually published a novel in monthly numbers or instalments; starting it, indeed, upon a plan, but often working at white heat to fulfil the next instalment, and improvising as he went. Thackeray used the same method, with the printer's devil ever infesting the hall when the day for delivery came around. This method of writing masterpieces may well daunt their successors, even in this journalistic age of internal combustion with the voice of Mr. H. G. Wells insistent that the faster anyone travels the nearer he is *ex hypothesi* to that New Jerusalem in which there shall be no night (and therefore, I presume, not a comfortable bed to be hired), but the eternal noise of elevators and daylight-saving made perfect. It did not daunt our forefathers: who were giants of their time, undertook a *Pendennis* or a *Dombey and Son*, and having accomplished a chapter or so, cheerfully went to bed and slept under that dreadful imminent duty. You all know, who have studied *Pickwick*, that *Pickwick* began (so to speak) in the air; that it took the narrative, so desultory in conception, some numbers before it found a plot at all. But how admirable is the plot, once found or—to say better—once happened on! For a double peripeteia who could ask better art than the charitable turn of Pickwick on Jingle in the debtor's prison, and the incarceration and release of Mrs. Bardell? Consider the first. Insensibly, without premonition of ours and I dare to say, of no long prepared purpose in the author, the story finds a climax:

"Come here, Sir," said Mr. Pickwick, trying to look stern, with four large tears running down his waistcoat. "Take that, Sir."

Take what? In the ordinary acceptation of such language, it should have been a blow. As the world runs, it ought to have been a sound hearty cuff: for Mr. Pickwick had been duped, deceived, and wronged by the destitute outcast who was now wholly in his power. Must we tell the truth? It was something from Mr. Pickwick's waistcoat pocket which chinked as it was given into Job's hand. . . .

But this admirable plot, with all the Bardell *versus* Pickwick business, and the second most excellent "reversal of fortune" when Mrs. Bardell, the prosecutrix, herself gets cast into prison by Dodson and Fogg whose tool she has been, and there, confronted by her victim and theirs, finds herself (O wonder!) pardoned—with the simple, sudden, surprising, yet most natural and (when you come to think of it) most Christian story of Sam Weller's loyalty and Mr. Weller's aiding and abetting, so absurdly and withal so delicately done—all this grew, as everyone knows, with the story's growth and grew out of fierce, rapid, improvisation. You can almost see the crucible with the fire under it, taking heat, reddening, exhaling fumes of milk-punch; and then, with Sam Weller and Jingle cast into it for ingredients, boiling up and precipitating the story, to be served

as a dish
Fit for the gods

—"served," not "carved." You cannot carve the dish of your true *improvisatore*. You cannot *articulate* a story of Dickens—or, if you can, "the less Dickens he": you may be sure it is one of his worst. *A Tale of Two Cities* has a deft plot: well-knit but stagey: and, I would add, stagey *because* well-knit, since (as we shall presently see) Dickens, cast back upon plot, ever conceived it in terms of the stage; of the stage, moreover, at its worst—of the early-Victorian stage, before even a Robertson had preluded better things. So, when I talk to any man of Dickens, and he ups with his first polite concession that *A Tale of Two Cities* is a fine story, anyhow, I know that man's case to be difficult, for that he admires what is least admirable in Dickens. Why, Gentlemen, you or I could with some pains construct as good a plot as that of *A Tale of Two Cities*; as you or I could with some pains construct a neater plot than Shakespeare invented for *The Merry Wives of Windsor* or even hand out some useful improvements

on the plot of *King Lear*. The trouble with us is that
we cannot write a *Merry Wives*, a *Lear*; cannot touch
that *it* which, achieved, sets the *Merry Wives* and *Lear*,
in their degrees, above imperfection, indifferent to
imperfections detectable even by a fool. Greatness is
indefinable, whether in an author or a man of affairs:
but had I to attempt the impossibility, no small part
of my definition would set up its rest on indifference—
on a grand carelessness of your past mistakes, involv-
ing a complete unconcern for those who follow them,
to batten on the bone you have thrown over your
shoulder.

II

Dickens was a great *novelist*—as I should contend,
the greatest of English novelists—and certainly among
the greatest of all the greatest European novelists.
His failing was that he did not quite trust his genius
for the novel, but was persuaded that it could be
bettered by learning from the drama—from the bad
drama of his time. But I want you to see, Gentlemen,
how honourable was the artist's endeavour; how
creditable, if mistaken, to the man. He was a born
improvisatore. *Pickwick*, under your eyes, takes a
shape—conceives it, finds it—as the story goes on.
Then shape he must struggle for; the idea of "shape"
has, against his genius, taken hold on him. So *Pickwick* is not finished before he begins a new story, never
thinking to repeat, by similar methods, *Pickwick's*
overwhelming success. No, the responsibility of that
success weighs on him; but it is a responsibility to
improve. The weakness of *Pickwick*, undertaken as
a series of mock-sporting episodes, lies in its desultori-

ness. This time we will have a well-knit plot. And
so we get *Oliver Twist* and *Nicholas Nickleby*, each with
any amount of plot, but of plot in the last degree
stagey; so stagey, indeed, that in *Nickleby* the critic
gasps at the complacency of an author who, having
created that "nurseling of immortality" Mr. Vincent
Crummles, together with a world and the atmosphere
of that world in which Crummles breathes and moves
and has his being, can work the strings of the puppet
with so fine a finger, detect its absurdities with so sure
an instinct and reveal them with so riotous a joy; yet
misses to see that he himself is committing absurdities
just as preposterous, enormities of the very same cate-
gory, on page after page. The story of Lord Frederick
Verisopht and Sir Mulberry Hawke, for example, is
right Crummles from beginning to end. Crummles
could have composed it in his sleep,—and to say this,
mind you, is to convey in the very censure an implicit
compliment—or, shall I use a more modest word and
say implicit homage? Crummles could have written a
great part of *Nickleby*: but Crummles could only have
written it after Dickens had made him. I seem to hear
the two arguing it out in some *Dialogue of the Dead.*

Auctor. "My dear Crummles, however *did* you contrive
to be what you are?"
Crummles. "Why, don't you see, Mr. Dickens? You
created me in your image." (*sotto voce*) "And, he doesn't
know it, poor great fellow, but it seems to me I've been
pretty smart in returning the compliment."

III

I have said, in a previous lecture, that Dickens, from
first to last, strove to make himself a better artist;

quoting to you a sentence of Henley's, which I repeat
here because you have almost certainly forgotten it:

He had in him at least as much of the French artist as
of the middle-class Englishman; and if in all his life, he
never ceased from self-education, but went unswervingly
in the pursuit of culture, it was out of love for his art and
because his conscience as an artist would not let him do
otherwise.

"Unswervingly"?—no, not unswervingly. No great
genius that ever was has marched unswervingly on.
As a condition of becoming a great artist he must be
more sensitive than his fellows; as a result of that sensitiveness he will doubt, hesitate, draw back to leap
the better. The very success of his latest book, his
latest picture, alarms him. "Oh yes," the true artist
says to his heart, "popularity is sweet; money is sweet;
and I can hold both in my hand by the simple process
of repeating myself." And the temptations are many
and great. You have on the profits of your first and
second books, and a reasonable hope of continuance,
enlarged your way of life, incurred responsibilities,
built a charming house not yet paid for, married a
wife who adores you (shall we say?) and is proud of
your celebrity, but for these very reasons—and chiefly
for love—will on any diminution of your fame, fret
secretly even if she does not nag actively. Against
this we have, opposed, the urge in the true artist who—
having done a thing—tosses it over his shoulder and
thinks no more of it; can only think of how to do
something further and do it better. I indicate the
strength of the temptation. There are, of course,
sundry ways of getting round it. For instance, as *I*
read the life of Shakespeare from the few hints left

to us, Shakespeare dodged it by the Gordian-knot solution of leaving his wife and bolting to London: a solution in this particular instance happy for us, yet not even on that account to be recommended in general to young literary aspirants. I mention Shakespeare here less for this, than as an exemplar of the true artist, never content with his best, to repeat it. Why, having written a *Hamlet*, an *Othello*, did he, instead of reproducing *Hamlets* and *Othellos*, go on to have a shy at a *Cymbeline*? For the self-same reason, Sirs, why Ulysses—if I may quote a poet none too popular just now—could not bide at home after even such tribulations of wandering as had become a proverb:

> I am become a name;
> For always roaming with a hungry heart
> Much have I seen and known; cities of men
> And manners, climates, councils, governments,
> Myself not least, but honour'd of them all;
> And drunk delight of battle with my peers,
> Far on the ringing plains of windy Troy.
> I am a part of all that I have met;
> Yet all experience is an arch wherethro'
> Gleams that untravell'd world, whose margin fades
> For ever and for ever when I move.
> How dull it is to pause, to make an end,
> To rust unburnish'd, not to shine in use!
> As tho' to breathe were life. Life piled on life
> Were all too little, and of one to me
> Little remains: but every hour is saved
> From that eternal silence, something more,
> A bringer of new things—

You may read the mere yearning of this, if you will, in Defoe, opening *The Further Adventures of Robinson Crusoe*; or, if you will, in Kipling's

> For to admire an' for to see,
>   For to be'old this world so wide—
> It never done no good to me,
>   But I can't drop it if I tried

—and these express the *instinct*.   The sanction, for us, lies in the words

> but every hour is saved
> From that eternal silence, something more,
> A bringer of new things.

And the desire for that—as I am sure you know—operates with no less force of prompting in the spiritual world than in the world of commerce and sea-travel. It carried Shakespeare at the last to that Ariel's isle which no commentator has ever (thank heaven!) been able yet to locate; and it brought him home at the very last

> A bringer of new things.

IV

Now if you accept no more than a much lower estimate of Dickens than I am preaching, you will be apt to dismiss what I have just been saying as "tall talk": and you will be quite mistaken, because it applies from Shakespeare down to men of infinitesimally less desert than Dickens; to every small artist, in fact, whose conscience will not cease harrying him until he improves on his best: a process which obviously—and, as a matter of history, with the great authors—never stops until they come to the grave.

At which point my now notorious discursiveness,

Gentlemen, also stops and gets back to Dickens. You see, the trouble of the matter is that in these experiments an author can never be sure. He takes an infinite risk, it may be *against his own true genius.* Where is the critic to correct him?

V

Well, with Dickens, his own adoring public corrected him sharply and, on the whole, with true instinct. To them he was the wand-waving magician, the *improvisatore in excelsis* who had caught up out of their midst an elderly small gentleman in spectacles and gaiters and shot him suddenly out of Goswell Street into the firmament, to be a star equal with Hercules—

sic fratres Helenae, lucida sidera—

"instead of which" he had turned to making plots so patently theatrical (and of the theatre of Crummles) that the man himself was helping everybody to see through them. So came the revenge; over-proved by the opening chapter of *Martin Chuzzlewit,* which I suppose to be about the sorriest piece of writing ever perpetrated by a great English writer. Its perusal induces on *me* at any rate, something like physical misery, not unmixed with the sort of shame any one of us might feel if a parent behaved unbecomingly in public. I want to obey the exhortation on Mrs. Sapsea's monument and "with a blush retire."

But, note you, the general reader—that entity often abused, seldom quite the fool that he looks—was quick to mark and punish. Listen to Forster:

Chuzzlewit had fallen short of all the expectations formed of it in regard to sale. By much the most masterly of his writings hitherto, the public had rallied to it in far less numbers than to any of its predecessors. . . . The primary cause of this, there is little doubt, had been the change to weekly issues in the form of publication of his last two stories. . . . The forty and fifty thousand purchasers of *Pickwick* and *Nickleby*, the sixty and seventy thousand of the early numbers of the enterprises in which *The Old Curiosity Shop* and *Barnaby Rudge* appeared had fallen to little over twenty thousand. They rose, somewhat on Martin's ominous announcement, at the end of the fourth number, that he'd go to America. . . .

They rose at once by a couple of thousand: but a serial of course can never be easily lifted out of a rut into which it has once dropped. The reasons for this are obvious, and the serial sales of *Chuzzlewit* never overtopped twenty-three thousand. There was a very different story when *Chuzzlewit* came to book form. "Its sale, since," writes Forster, "has ranked next after *Pickwick* and *Copperfield*." In short, Dickens had been, quite conscientiously, in the opening chapters of *Chuzzlewit*, working against the grain of his genius. His public recalled him to it in the brutal way the public uses. When he sat down to write *Chuzzlewit* he had never an idea of carrying Martin off to America. Suddenly, in fear of falling sales and many challenges to make good his *American Notes*, he became the *improvisatore* again and switched his hero across the Atlantic. Who will deny that the American chapters of *Martin Chuzzlewit* are its best and, save for any given chapter upon which Sarah Gamp knocks in, its most memorable?

VI

None the less, and to the end, Dickens the artist is hag-ridden by this business of "plot," which for him meant "stage-plot." It hampers him in book after book, as its silly exigencies perpetually get in the way of the reader's pleasure, even of the reader's understanding. His genius did not lie that way, any more than did Shakespeare's. I put in this comparison, for it can never be untimely for a Professor of English Literature to get in a word to damn the school-books which present Shakespeare to you as chasing along his shelves for some Italian novel to provide him with a new plot. Oh, believe me, Gentlemen—after *The Comedy of Errors* and that sort of thing, Shakespeare never bothered any more about his plots or whence he took them. It is very right indeed for a young author to sweat his soul over "plot" structure. But, through practice, there comes a time—suddenly, it may be, but as sure in his development as puberty in his physical growth—when lo! he has a hundred plots to his hand, if heaven would but grant him time to treat them. I often wonder why men blame the elder Dumas so severely, accepting the allegation that he employed hirelings—viciously termed by the critic his "ghosts" or his "devils." Why, if you have an imagination teeming, like Dumas', with stories to make men happier—*why*, knowing how short is life and that you cannot, on this side of the grave, tell one-fifth of these with your own pen—why go to that grave leaving the world, through that scruple, so much imaginatively the poorer? Only the thing should be done frankly, openly, of course.

VII

I just raise that question. It applies to Dumas and (I think) to most great novelists. But it applies less to Dickens than to most—than to Trollope for instance. And in this very inapplicability lies a secret of Dickens' weakness which I am to suggest.

His plots are not merely stagey, melodramatic. Carefully examined, they are seen to repeat themselves, under a wealth of disguise, with an almost singular poverty of invention. Let us take one most favourite trick of his—the trick of "the masked battery" as I shall call it: the discomfiture of the villain by the betrayal of his supposed confederate. The characters are artfully assembled for the bad man's triumph. Of a sudden the confederate rounds on him, gives him away before the audience—usually in a long story, at the end of which the baffled schemer creeps away, usually again to destroy himself. We get this *coup* as early as in *Oliver Twist* where Monks blurts out his story. It is repeated in *Nickleby* when Ralph Nickleby is confronted with the man "Snawley" and by Squeers. In the next novel, *Martin Chuzzlewit*, we get a double dose; Jonas "given away" by an accomplice; Pecksniff explosively denounced by Old Chuzzlewit after a long course of watchful dissimulation. This idea of a long and careful dissimulation so catches hold of Dickens that he goes on to rope into its service in subsequent stories two men who, on his own showing of them, are about the very last two in the world capable of carrying through a strategy so patient—Mr. Micawber in *David Copperfield* and Mr. Boffin in *Our Mutual Friend*. As a portrait, Mr. Boffin ranks pretty high even in Dickens' gallery, while Micawber ranks with the very best of his best. But who will assert that either of them could have found it in his nature to behave as the plot compels them to behave? To continue—by just the same trick Quilp gets his exposure in *The Old Curiosity Shop*, Harewood forces the revelation in *Barnaby Rudge*, Lady Dedlock is hunted down in *Bleak House*. The more the peripeteia—the reversal of fortune—disguises itself, the more it is the same thing.

VIII

George Santayana—he is so excellent a writer that I dispense with "Doctor" or "Professor" or other prefix to his name—tells us that:

Dickens entered the theatre of this world by the stage door; the shabby little adventures of the actors in their private capacity replace for him the mock tragedies which they enact before a dreaming public. Mediocrity of circumstance and mediocrity of soul for ever return to the centre of his stage; a more wretched or a grander existence is sometimes broached, but the pendulum swings back, and we return, with the relief with which we put on our slippers after the most romantic excursion, to a golden mediocrity —to mutton and beer, and to love and babies in a suburban villa with one frowsy maid.

Yes, that is true enough, but not all the truth. Dickens entered the theatre by the stage door; but he passed through to the front, to turn up the lights, wave his wand and create a new world—a fairy world, let us agree: a theatrical world, as I have been attempting to show. Yet consider—

Most of us in this room have childish recollections of green fields, running brooks, woods in leaf, birds' nests, cattle at pasture, all that pageant of early summer which is going on at this moment a few furlongs from this desk—this dead piece of timber—and at the thought of which (if you will not think me impolite) I long to be somewhere else at this moment. With some of us elders, not specially imaginative, the early habit persists even after long servitude to city life: so that still by habit our first instinct on rising from bed is to go to the window and con the weather—how the day is making, from what quarter the wind sets—"Is it too strong for the fruit blossom?" "Will it be a good day for the trout?" Again, of my experience I appeal to some of you—to those who, aware in childhood or boyhood (quite suddenly, it may be, made aware) of the beauty underlying this world (yes, and clothing it too), have been as suddenly afflicted with the hopeless yearning to express it, was not that yearning awakened, quickened in you, you knew not how, by some casual sight—an open glade between woods, a ship with all canvas spread, or, through the hazels,

the nesting throstle's shining eye,

or the fish darting in the deep of a pool? Was it not some similar moment that, though you have never yet arrived at putting it and its underthought into words, yet so touched you that for the rest of your days you will understand what was in Coleridge's heart when he wrote:

O happy living things! no tongue
    Their beauty might declare:
A spring of love gush'd from my heart,
    And I blessed them unaware.

Yes, and I dare say your first visit to the theatre brought you a like delicious shock. (I can recall to this day, very distinctly, the gods and goddesses who, between the acts of my first pantomime, danced on the blue ceiling with baskets and festoons of roses.)

But now, bethink you that Dickens struggled through a childhood to which green fields, trees, birds, cattle, brooks and pools, were all denied: that the child was condemned to a squalid lodging; to spend his days washing bottles in a dreadful blacking factory, his hours "off" in visiting his parents in the yet more dreadful Marshalsea prison to which his father had been committed for debt: and you will understand not only that he had to enter the theatre of this world by the stage door, but that the lighted theatre, when he could pay a few pence and get to the gallery, was his one temple of beauty: that only there—if we except a hint or two picked up in the street—from a shabby acrobat or a stray Punch and Judy show—could he drink the romance for which his young spirit thirsted. You have all read, I doubt not, Charles Lamb's paper on "*My First Play*," first contributed to the *London Magazine* in December, 1821, afterwards reprinted in *Elia*:

But when we got in, and I beheld the green curtain that veiled a heaven to my imagination, which was soon to be disclosed—the breathless anticipations I endured! I had seen something like it in the plate prefixed to *Troilus and Cressida* in Rowe's Shakespeare—the tent scene with Diomede—and a sight of that plate can always bring back in a measure the feeling of that evening—The boxes at that time, full of well-dressed women of quality, projected over the pit; and the pilasters reaching down were adorned with a glistering substance (I know not what)

under glass (as it seemed), resembling—a homely fancy—
but I judged it to be sugar-candy—yet, to my raised imagination, divested of its homelier qualities, it appeared a
glorified candy!—The orchestra lights at length arose, those
'fair Auroras'! Once the bell sounded. It was to ring out
yet once again—and, incapable of anticipation, I reposed
my shut eyes in a sort of resignation upon the maternal
lap. It rang the second time. The curtain drew up—I
was not past six years old—and the play was Artaxerxes!

There we have the confession of a Cockney-bred boy,
more happily placed than was Dickens at the same age
or for many years later. Lamb had his hardships, his
tragedy or tragedies, in life: but in the childhood of
Dickens, most sensitively resentful, penury and shame-
ful occupation bit down to the bone. What other vision
of beauty had he—a born actor, as all contemporaries
report—but that which Drury Lane or Covent Garden
supplied? Love, says a late Roman singer, was born
in a *field*:

Ipse Amor, puer Dionae, rure natus dicitur—
Pleasure planteth a field; it conceives under Pleasure, the
    pang of its joy:
In a field was Dione in labour delivered of Cupid the boy:
And the field to her lap, to her fostering breast, took the
    rascal; he drew
Mother's milk from the delicate kisses of flowers and he
    prospered and grew—
Now learn ye to love who loved never: now ye who have
    loved, love anew!

The bad early and mid-Victorian stage hurt more
than one Victorian novelist of genius. It seriously
hurt Charles Reade, for example, who habitually sought
the advice of Egeria from a fourth-rate actress: and

that should bring tears to the eyes of any critic who knows Reade's strong country nurture and has sized his genius. But, with Dickens—think of that forlorn child, plotting to snatch his soul's sustenance in the shilling gallery of Drury Lane—at intervals how rare! Is it any wonder that—to convert a famous phrase— coming to power, he invoked out of the theatre a new world, to redress the balance of his old?

IX

Moreover—and mind you this—you will never understand Charles Dickens until you realise how exquisitely, how indignantly the genius in this child of the blacking-warehouse felt the shame of its lot. Dickens was never a snob: but a prouder spirit never inhabited flesh. This shepherd boy was not one to sing in the Valley of Humiliation. For years after success came to him he kept his mouth closed like a steel trap upon past agonies. At length he confided something to Forster (*Life*, Volume 1, Chapter 2), and few sadder reflections have ever been implied by a grown man upon his parents:

It is wonderful to me how I could have been so easily cast away at such an age. It is wonderful to me that, even after my descent into the poor little drudge I had been since we came to London, no one had compassion on me—a child of singular abilities, quick, eager, delicate, and soon hurt bodily or mentally—to suggest that something might have been spared, as certainly it might have been, to place me at any common school. Our friends, I take it, were tired out. No one made any sign. My father and mother were quite satisfied. They could hardly have been more so if I had been twenty years of age, distinguished at a Grammar School, and going to Cambridge.

Terrible words those: the more terrible for being, after long repression, uttered so judicially.

And again:

I suppose my lodging was paid for by my father: I certainly did not pay it myself, and I certainly had no other assistance whatever—the making of my clothes, I think, excepted—from Monday morning until Saturday night. No advice, no counsel, no encouragement, no consolation, no support, from anyone that I can call to mind, so help me God!

Nor did his parents' neglect end with starving his heart's affection, his brain's activity. It starved the weak little body into spasms through malnutrition. He had a boy friend in the warehouse, one Bob Fagin. Dickens writes of this time:

Bob Fagin was very good to me on the occasion of a bad attack of my old disorder. I suffered such excruciating pain that they made a temporary bed of straw in my old recess in the counting-house, and I rolled about on the floor, and Bob filled empty blacking-bottles with hot water, and applied relays of them to my side half the day. I got better and quite easy towards evening; but Bob (who was much bigger and older than I) did not like the idea of my going home alone, and took me under his protection. *I was too proud to let him know about the prison;* and after making several efforts to get rid of him, to all of which Bob Fagin in his goodness was deaf, shook hands with him on the steps of a house near Southwark Bridge on the Surrey side, making believe that I lived there. As a finishing piece of reality, in case of his looking back, I knocked at the door, I recollect, and asked, when the woman opened it, was that Mr. Robert Fagin's house?

O caeca pectora!   Dickens had hard streaks in him, and I confess to a curious wonderment how, afterwards, he could have used that name of Fagin—how he *could* have used it as he did—in *Oliver Twist*.

But I end by repeating my question—Is it any wonder that this street-boy of genius, coming to his own, invoked out of the theatre a new world, to redress the balance of his old?

Of that new world I propose to say something, Gentlemen, a fortnight hence.

DICKENS (IV)

PREFACE

I THINK it meet, Gentlemen, that before we resume our subject to-day, a word should be said on a loss that has befallen English letters in general and our sister-University in particular, since I last addressed you.

Walter Raleigh was an authentic son of Cambridge: and although he spent the most of his life teaching in other places the better understanding of a literature—our own literature—which in his undergraduate days had not found adqeuate recognition here, yet Cambridge had been his pasture, and he carried everywhere the mettle of that pasture: yes, and unmistakably, and although by the gay sincerity of his nature he would win men to like him, wherever he went.

Personal affection may count for too much in my faith that he will some day be recognised, not only for a true son of Cambridge, but for a great one in his generation. I put, however, that reckoning on one side. He did, very gaily and manfully and well, all the work that fell to his hand; and his end was in this wise. He had, in the first and second weeks of August, 1914, been eye-witness at Oxford of one of two amazing scenes —the other simultaneously passing here—when in these precincts, in these courts of unconscious preparation, by these two sacred streams, all on a sudden the spirit of youth was a host incorporate.

62

Χρυσῷ δ' ἄρα Δῆλος ἅπασα
ἤνθησ', ὡς ὅτε τε ῥίον οὔρεος ἄνθεσιν ὕλης.

"Then Delos broke in gold, as a mountain spur is canopied in season with the flowering bush."

"The mettle of your pasture" . . . "Multitudes, multitudes in the valley of decision" . . . and the host, so suddenly gathered, as suddenly in motion, gone, for their country's sake challenging the scythe. Raleigh saw that with his eyes, and could not forget.

The Dean of St. Paul's returned, the other day, to a rightly respectful Cambridge, to deliver a Rede Lecture to us on *The Victorian Age*. Now he is a fool who denies or doubts Dean Inge to be a great man of our time—though he may now and then be a little too apt to regard himself as the only widow of another. Dean Inge, at any rate, felt himself strong enough to tell you he had no doubt that, to the historian of the future, the Elizabethan and Victorian Ages will appear as "the twin peaks in which English civilisation culminated."

Now I have been talking to you—already through three lectures—upon the best-beloved writer of that Victorian Age—its most representative writer, perhaps —and preaching his eminence. But I should be nervous of claiming quite all that! It seems to me, if I may put it so without offence, a somewhat complacent view for *us* to take of an Age in which we were born— he, to unseal the vials of prophecy, I, just to happen along with the compensation of a more sanguine temperament. He admits that he has "no wish to offer an unmeasured panegyric on an age which after all cannot be divested of the responsibility for making our own inevitable." He admits that "the twentieth century will doubtless be full of interest, and may even develop some elements of greatness." But as regards this country, "the signs are that our work on a grand scale, with the whole world as our stage, is probably nearing its end." Well, I dare to say that such talk from a man of the Dean's age or mine is more than unhopeful; is ungrateful:

Difficilis, querulus, laudator temporis acti. . . .

Would he but go back in memory to the *tempus actum* of August, 1914, it may dawn upon him that "fears may be liars" and the likelier for that some hopes were not dupes: that some men less gifted, less eloquent, than he, in those August days of 1914 saw this vision as of a farther Pacific:

Silent, upon a peak in Darien.

Raleigh at any rate saw it: I would not use extravagant language, but I verily believe Raleigh, from that hour, saw the assembled chivalry of those boys of 1914 as a meadow of cloth-of-gold spreading past all known or prophetical horizons—a prairie, the scent over which was a scent of sacrifice, at once holy and intolerable. Let me repeat—for one does not ring changes on the loss of a friend—the mourning bell strikes once and repeats itself—let me repeat some words written, the other night, under durance on returning from his funeral:

In his last few years, under an invincible inward compulsion, he turned from his life's trade, in which he had vindicated himself as one of the best few, to become a child again and learn to be a valiant soldier. The sacrifice of the young in 1914–18, about which so many talk so easily, was a torture to him: it cut to the bone, the marrow. It was matter for indignation that he should survive these many boys. . . . Some of us, who noted, almost from the first, the operation of the War upon Raleigh's soul, foreboded that in some way or other it would cut short his span, or, at least, that it menaced him. His converse again and again would wander away from the old writers, once his heart-fellows, to machinery, air-fights, anything. . . . When I last talked with him he was full of his History of the Air Service in the War, the first volume of which is in the press, I believe. For the second he went out to survey, from the air, the fields of campaign in Mesopotamia, took typhoid in Baghdad, and came home just in time to die.

It is a purely simple story: of a great teacher who saw his pupils go from him on a call more instant than his teaching, and followed their shades with no thought of

So were I equall'd with them in renown

but the thought only to overtake them in service.

Forgive the length of my discourse, Gentlemen. It is right, I think, that our sister-Universities should feel one for the other's pride, one for the other's wound.

I

To take up our tale—
It has already been objected against these lectures on Dickens—or against such parts of them as the news-

papers honour me by quoting—that they treat **Dickens** as a genius of the first class. That term has little meaning for me who seldom or never think—can hardly bring myself to think—of great men in class-lists, in terms of a Tripos. (I reserve that somewhat crude method of criticism to practise it upon those who are *going to be* great men; and even so—if you will credit me—derive scant enjoyment from it.) But I foresaw the objection, and forestalled it by quoting a famous saying of Tasso, and I take my stand on that: as I take not the smallest interest in weighing Chaucer against Pope, Shakespeare against Milton, Scott against Burns, or Dickens against Thackeray. Chaucer, Shakespeare, Scott, Dickens—their other qualities apart—are grand creators, lords of literature all, by this specific virtue; and, were there sense in challenging, with this *quadriga* alone we could securely challenge any literature in any living tongue. Note you, moreover: it is to this creative power that other artists less creative, but great and therefore generous, instinctively pay homage: Dryden, for instance, or Byron:

> 'Tis to create, and in creating live
> A being more intense that we endow
> With form our fancy, gaining as we give
> The life we image, even as I do now.
> What am I? Nothing: but not so art thou,
> Soul of my thought! . . .
>
> (*Childe Harold*, iii. 6.)

Or again:

> The mind can make
> Substance, and people planets of its own
> With beings brighter than have been, and give
> A breath to forms which can outlive all flesh. . . .
>
> (*The Dream*, st. 1.)

Note you particularly, if you will, the words "planets of its own. . . ." We talk too often, perhaps (I have talked in this fashion myself unheedingly), as if these men had been makers of picture-galleries, lining their walls with lively characters, brilliant portraits. But in truth neither Chaucer's *Prologue* nor Shakespeare's succession of women, neither *Redgauntlet* nor *David Copperfield*, is a gallery of characters; but a planet rather, with its own atmosphere which the characters breathe; in which as proper inhabitants they move easily and have their natural being: while for us all great literature is a catholic hostelry, in which we seat ourselves at the board with Falstaff, Dugald Dalgetty, Sam Weller, the Wife of Bath, Mrs. Gamp and Mrs. Quickly, and wonder how soon Don Quixote, My Uncle Toby, or The Three Musketeers will knock in to share the good meat and the wine.

II

So, between a discussion of Dickens' plots—which we examined a fortnight ago and found wanting—at once stagey and ill-knit and, at that, repetitive, poor in invention; and of his characters, which teemed from his brain in a procession closed only by their author's death, so inexhaustibly various and withal so individual, vivid and distinct, that the critic can scarcely help telling himself, "Here, and only here, *must* lie the secret of the man's genius"; I shall interpose to-day a few words upon this world of Dickens, with its atmosphere.

For it is a strange world, with an atmosphere of its own, as strange as itself.

I have already noted some things of that world of his—that it was a crowded world: a world of the city, of the streets; that his novels, when they visit the country, take us at a violent rate in post-chaises to find, with Shenstone,

The warmest welcome at an inn.

For one moment, at the term of Little Nell's wanderings, in the quiet of the old schoolmaster's garden, we almost touch a sense of country rest and repose. But of *real* country, of solid growth in rest, of sport, of gardens, of farms and tenantry, of harvests, of generations rooted, corroborated in old grudges, old charities; of all that England stood for in Dickens' day and, of its sap, fed what Cobbett had already called the "Great Wen" of London, our author had about as much sense as Mr. Winkle of a horse, or a snipe.

Now I wish to be rather particularly scrupulous just here: for we are dealing with a peculiarly, an unmistakably genuine, English writer; who, himself a child of the streets, acquainted, by eyesight and daily wont, with an industrial England into which the old agricultural England—what with railway and factory, gas, and everything extractible from coal—was rapidly converting itself; did yet by instinct seize on the ancient virtues. Take away the hospitality, the punch and mistletoe, from Dingley Dell, and what sort of a country house is left? Why, the *Handley Cross* series, for which Messrs. Chapman and Hall intended *Pickwick* as a stale challenge, could give *Pickwick* ten and a beating from the first. As the season comes round you play cricket at Dingley Dell, or you skate, or you mix the bowl and turn the toe. But the stubble-fields are not there, nor the partridges; nor the turnips, nor the gallops to hounds, nor the tillage and reaping, nor the drowsed evenings with tired dogs a-stretch by the hearth. Of all this side of England Dickens knew, of acquaintance, nothing. I am not speaking, you will understand, of any Wordsworthian intimacy with natural scenery tender or sublime, of anything imparted or suggested to the imagination by a primrose or in the "sounding cataract" haunting it "like a passion." I am speaking rather of human life as lived in rural England in Dickens' time and in some corners yet surviving the week-end habit. Of these Sabine virtues, of these Sabine amenities and hardships, of the countryman's eye on the weather-glass for "snow and vapours, wind and storm, fulfilling His word," Dickens (I repeat) had no sense, having no tradition, of field life, of that *neighbourliness* which existed in quiet places and persisted around ancient houses:

> The summer air of this green hill
> 'Va-heaved in bosoms now all still,
> And all their hopes and all their tears
> Be unknown things of other years. . . .
> So, if 'twere mine, I'd let alone
> The great old House of mossy stone.

Dickens loved the old stage-coaches and travel by them. What he thought of the new railways and their effect upon landscape, you may read in *Dombey and Son*. He lived, moreover, to undergo the chastening experience of a railway collision. But his actual sense of the country you may translate for yourself from the account, in *Bleak House*, of the country life of Sir Leicester and Lady Dedlock. It is worse than stupid: it is vapid: or, rather, it is not there at all. Will you conceive Dickens, closing one of those Adelphi-Dedlock chapters and running his head suddenly into Mr. Wilfrid Blunt's ballad of *The Old Squire*?

> I like the hunting of the hare
>   Better than that of the fox;
> The new world still is all less fair
>   Than the old world it mocks. . . .
>
> I leave my neighbours to their thought;
>   My choice it is, and pride,
> On my own lands to find my sport,
>   In my own fields to ride. . . .
>
> Nor has the world a better thing
>   Though one should search it round,
> Than thus to live, one's own sole king
>   Upon one's own sole ground.
>
> I like the hunting of the hare;
>   It brings me, day by day,
> The memory of old days as fair
>   With dead men past away.
>
> To these, as homeward still I ply
>   And pass the churchyard gate
> Where all are laid as I must lie,
>   I stop and raise my hat.
>
> I like the hunting of the hare;
>   New sports I hold in scorn.
> I like to be as my fathers were
>   In the days e'er I was born.

For a figure like that—hopelessly conservative, if you will, but conceived of truth, Dickens could only substitute a week-ender (as we should say nowadays) and make him a pompous ass. By one touch or two, of understanding what "the stately homes of England" really stood for—their virtue along with their stupidity—by one touch of Jane Austen's wit, shall we say?—Dickens might have made some sort of a fist of it. As it is, when he wanders anywhere into the country, he is a lost child, mooning incuriously along the hedgerows with an impercipience rivalling that of a famous Master of Trinity who once confessed that his ignorance of botany was conterminous with all Solomon's knowledge, since it ranged from the cedar of Lebanon to the hyssop that grows in the wall. Dickens' favourite flower (we have it on record) was a scarlet geranium!

Still, I would be fair, and must mention a fact which I have experimentally discovered for myself and tested of late in the slow process of compiling a Book of English Prose (an "Oxford Book," if you will forgive me), that, while our poetry from the very first—from "Sumer is icumen in; Lhude sing cuccu!"—positively riots in country scenes, sounds, scents, country delights:

—all foison, all abundance,

and soothes us with the deep joy of it, with music and "the herb called heart's-ease," of all such joy, even of all such perception, our prose, until we come to the middle of the last century, is correspondently barren. Consider what a unique thing, and unique for generations, was *The Compleat Angler*! Try of your memory to match it. An Essay of Temple's? a few pages of Bunyan, of Evelyn? The Sir Roger de Coverly papers?—charming; but of the town, surely, and with something of Saturday-to-Monday patronage not only in pose but in *raison d'être*? Fielding understood the country better—witness his Squire Allworthy. But

on the whole, and in fairness, if Dickens' pages exhibit—
and they do—a thin theatrical picture of rural England,
without core or atmosphere, against his childhood's
disinheritance—against the mean streets and the
Marshalsea—we must balance (if I may use a para-
doxical term) the weight of traditional vacuity.

III

But I fear we have a great deal more to empty out
of this world of his.

To begin with, we must jettison religion; or at any
rate all religion that gets near to definition by words in
a *Credo*. Religious formulae I think we may say that
he hated; and equally that he had little use for ministers
of religion. I can recall but one sympathetic portrait
of an Anglican parson—the Reverend Septimus Crisparkle, Minor Canon of Cloisterham—and that in
his last book, and with scarcely a shadow of a quality
impinged upon it by his vocation, by Holy Orders:
Crisparkle, Minor Canon and muscular Christian, well
visualised, is a good fellow just as Tartar in the same
story is a good fellow: nothing more. George Eliot and
Charlotte Brontë, who disliked ecclesiastics, have to
give them understanding, even sympathy, in some
degree. Dickens merely neglects them. Unaccredited
missionaries of the Gospel are humbugs all, in Dickens;
uneducated Pharisees, Stiggins's, Chadbands; devourers
of widows' (and widowers') houses; spongers on the
kindness and credulity of poor folk just a little more
ignorant than they, while far more innocent. As for
sacred edifices—cathedrals, churches—Dickens uses
them as picturesque, romantic, mouldy, just as suits his
convenience—a last harbourage for Little Nell or an

object with a steeple suggesting to Mr. Wemmick—
"Hullo! here's a church! . . . let's get married!"
If Dickens ever conceives of a church as a tabernacle
of any faith, I have yet to find the passage.

You must remember that, while Dickens wrote,
Tractarian Movements, Unitarian Movements, Posi-
tivist Movements—Wiseman's claim, Newman's se-
cession, the Gorham judgment, Bishop Colenso's
heresies—Darwin's hypothesis, Huxley's agnostic re-
jection of doctrine, and so on—that all these were
agitating men's thoughts as with a succession of shocks
of earthquake. But all these passed Dickens by, as
little observed as felt by him: simply disregarded.

IV

Of political thought, again, his world is almost as
empty. He was, in his way, an early-Victorian Radical.
When he saw a legal or political hardship which hurt
or depressed the poor, conventions injurious to the
Commonwealth—the Poor Laws, Debtors' Prisons, the
Court of Chancery, the Patent (or Circumlocution)
Office and so forth, with the people who batten on such
conventions, taking them for granted as immutable—
Dickens struck hard and often effectively. But he
struck at what he saw under his own eyes. Beyond
this immediate indignation he had no reasoned principles of political or social reform. I have to hand, at
this moment, no evidence to confirm a guess which I
will nevertheless hazard, that he hated Jeremy Bentham
and all his works. Certainly the professional, bullying,
committee-working philanthropists—Mrs. Jellaby and
Mr. Honeythunder, whose successors pullulate in this age
—were the very devil to him. His simple formula ever

was—in an age when Parliament carried a strong tradition of respect—"Yes, my Lords and Gentlemen, look on this waif, this corpse, this broken life. Lost, broken, dead, my Lords and Gentlemen, and all through your acquiescence, your misfeasance, your neglect!" To the immediate reader his message ran simply, "Take into your heart God's most excellent gift of Charity: by which I mean let Charity begin at home, in that kingdom of God which is within you, let it operate in your own daily work; let it but extend to your own neighbours who need your help; and so—and only so—will the city of God be established on earth."

V

I perceive, Gentlemen, that in my hurry I have let slip a great part of the secret, and so will add but this in hasty summary, catching up, before retreat, my cloak of *advocatus diaboli:*

(1) In the first place, Dickens' world was not a world of ideas at all, but a city "full of folk." Compared with the world as Carlyle saw it, or Clough, or Martineau, or Newman, or Arnold, it is void of ideas, if not entirely unintellectual.

(2) Moreover, and secondly, it is a vivid hurrying world; but the characters in it—until you come to Pip, say, in *Great Expectations*—are all quite curiously static; and, as the exception proves the rule, I am not afraid to back this assertion against *Martin Chuzzlewit*, for example, in which young Martin is, of set purpose, to be converted out of the family selfishness. Things happen to Mr. Pecksniff, to Little Nell, to Mr. Micawber, to Mr. Dombey, to Bradley Headstone and Eugene Wraybourne, to Sally Brass and her brother: but, *as*

the rule, these things do not happen *within them*, as such things happen in the soul of any protagonist in a novel by Tolstoy or Dostoievsky, or as they are intended and traced as happening (say) in *Romola*. Dombey's conversion is a mere stage-trick; and, for Micawber's apotheosis as a prosperous colonist, let him believe it who will.

VI

Further—and to conclude on this point—over and beyond its infertility of thought, Dickens' is a world in which technical or professional skill never comes into play to promote anything on earth. We have spoken of his clergy. His innumerous lawyers, from the Lord Chancellor to Messrs. Dodson and Fogg (assisted by his own personal experience in the Law's service), draw their money for exculpating the guilty or slowly killing the righteous through hope deferred:

> The oppressor's wrong, the proud man's contumely,
> The pangs of dispriz'd love, the law's delay,
> The insolence of office—

Equally with lawyers (readers of epitaphs and of *David Copperfield* will take the allusion) "physicians are in vain." It would be interesting [I do not suggest it as a subject of research for a Ph.D. degree] to count the number of births in Dickens' novels and discover an *accoucheur* who did not contrive to lose either the mother or the child, or both.

VII

What remains, then, of a world thus emptied of religion, thought, science?

I reserve the answer for a minute or two.

But I start my approach to it thus: Be the world of Dickens what you will, he had the first demiurgic gift, of entirely believing in what he created. The belief may be as frantic as you will: for any true artist it is the first condition. Well, this remains: nobody has ever doubted that, in the preface to *David Copperfield*, he wrote the strict truth:

It would concern the reader little, perhaps, to know how sorrowfully the pen is laid down at the end of a two-years' imaginative task; or how an Author feels as if he were dismissing some portion of himself into the shadowy world, when a crowd of all the creatures of his brain are going from him forever. Yet I had nothing else to tell, unless indeed I were to confess (which might be of less moment still) that no one can ever believe this Narrative in the reading more than I believed it in the writing.

Well, there, Gentlemen—just there, and so simply— you have the first condition of a work of art—its own creator is so possessed that he thoroughly believes in it. As Henry James once said to me (I recall the words as nearly as I can), "Ah, yes, how jollily the little figures dance under the circle of the lamp, until *Good-bye*, and off they go, to take their chance of the dark!"

VIII

Having that, you have artistic sincerity: of which I wonder, as experience enlarges, how many faults it cannot excuse—or indeed *what is the fault it cannot excuse*.

All that remains of the merely artistic secret has been summarised by Mr. Saintsbury:

It cannot have taken many people of any competence in criticism very long to discover where, at least in a general way, the secret of this "new world" of Dickens lies. *It lies, of course, in the combination of the strictest realism of detail with a fairy-tale unrealism of general atmosphere.* The note of one or the other or both, is sometimes forced and then there is a jar: in the later books this is frequently the case. But in *Pickwick* it hardly ever occurs; and therefore, to all happily fit persons, the "suspension of disbelief," to adopt and shift Coleridge's great dictum from verse to prose fiction, is, except in the case of some of the short inset stories, never rudely broken. Never, probably, was there a writer who knew or cared less about Aristotle than Dickens did. If he had spoken of the father of criticism, he would probably have talked—one is not certain that he has not sometimes come near to talking—some of his worst stuff. But certainly, when he did master it (which was often) nobody ever mastered better than Dickens, in practice, the Aristotelian doctrine of the impossibility rendered probable or not improbable.

Well, there you have the artistic secret of Dickens' world accurately given, and not by me. *It lies in the combination of the strictest realism of detail with a fairy-tale unrealism of general atmosphere.*

Let me give you, to illustrate this, a single instance out of many. In his Christmas story, *The Perils of Certain English Prisoners*—an adventurous story of the sort that Stevenson loved and some of you make the mistake of despising—a handful of a British garrison with their women and children in a stockaded fort in South America tensely await an attack of pirates hopelessly outnumbering them. Now listen to one paragraph:

(It is a corporal of Marines who tells it.)

"Close up here, men, and gentlemen all!" said the sergeant. "A place too many in the line."

The pirates were so close upon us at this time that the foremost of them were already before the gate. More and more came up with a great noise, and shouting loudly. When we believed from the sound that they were all there, we gave three English cheers. The poor little children joined, and were so fully convinced of our being at play, that they enjoyed the noise, and were heard clapping their hands in the silence that followed.

Defoe within his limits does that sort of thing to perfection: but then Defoe's world observes the limits of the "real" (as we absurdly call everything that is not spiritual), has little emotion, scintillates scarce a glimmer of humour. Dickens handles it in a phantasmagoric world, charged even to excess with emotion, and is not in the least afraid to employ it—I quote Mr. Saintsbury again:

Of invading those confines of nonsense which Hazlitt proudly and wisely claimed as the appanage and province of every Englishman.

I need but to instance a writer whose acquaintance Hazlitt had not the joy to make, nor Lamb—woe upon these divisions of time!—Lewis Carroll, in whom both would have revelled for his insane logicality of detail— or, if you prefer it, I will fall back upon Lear's Nonsense Books or even upon *A Midsummer-Night's Dream*—to convince you that, as a nation, we have this appanage: and if it bewilder a foreigner, or he deride it, why then we will give him a look, and pass.

IX

Yes, but there is something else.

What else—no mere artistic secret—ties this phantasmagoric world to ours and makes it universal with ours, conterminous, and so real?

It is no dodge or trick of artistry that can work so incredible a feat—that can open our hearts to such beings as Dick Swiveller and Mrs. Gamp (whom in private life you or I would avoid like the plague)—to enjoy their company, to hang on every word they utter. It must be some very simple catholic gift, thus to unite the unreal with the real, thus to make brothers and sisters of all men and women, high or low.

It is: nor shall I delay you by elaborate pretence to search for it. For I know; and you know, or will recognise it as soon as I utter the word. It is *Charity*; the inestimable gift of Charity that Dickens flings over all things as his magic mantle: so that, whether there be prophecies, they shall fail; whether there be tongues, they shall cease; whether there be knowledge, it shall vanish away; and whether there be little critics tormented about Dickens' style, in the folds of that mantle they shall be folded and hushed:

That it may please Thee to preserve all that travel by land or by water, all women labouring of child, sick persons, and young children; and to shew Thy pity upon all prisoners and captives.

That it may please Thee to defend, and provide for, the fatherless children, and widows, and all that are desolate and oppressed.

That is the last secret of Dickens: and *that* is what George Santayana means when he writes:

If Christendom should lose everything that is now in the melting-pot, human life would still remain amiable and quite adequately human. I draw this comforting assurance from the pages of Dickens.

DICKENS (V)

I

"I REMEMBER," says Henry James in a wise little
Essay on *The Art of Fiction*—

I remember an English novelist, a woman of genius,
telling me that she was much commended for the impression she had managed to give in one of her tales of the nature and way of life of the French Protestant youth. She
had been asked where she learned so much about this
recondite being, she had been congratulated on her peculiar
opportunities. These opportunities consisted in her having,
once, in Paris, as she ascended a staircase, passed an open
door where, in the household of a *pasteur*, some of the
young Protestants were seated at table round a finished
meal. The glimpse made a picture; it lasted only a moment, but that moment was experience.

I wish I could make you promise, Gentlemen, to bear
this little story in mind whenever some solemn fellow
assures you that a man rustically born and bred could
not have written *Hamlet* or *The Tempest*; "he would
never have seen this, learned or experienced that" and
so on: the simple answer being that under such disadvantage *they* would never have written *Hamlet* or
The Tempest. They are, in fact, not even Shakespeares
to the extent of understanding how an artist creates,
how the imaginative mind operates.

Henry James, who was an artist and understood that operation, simply comments on his anecdote that the lady had caught her direct personal impression and it was enough:

She knew what youth was, and what Protestantism: she also had the advantage of having seen what it was to be French, so that she converted these ideas into a concrete image and produced a reality.

Above all, however, she was blessed with the faculty which when you give it an inch takes an ell, and which for the artist is a much greater source of strength than any accident of residence or of place in the social scale. The power to guess the unseen from the seen, to trace the implication of things, to judge the whole piece by the pattern, the condition of feeling life in general so completely that you are well on your way to knowing any particular corner of it—this cluster of gifts may almost be said to constitute experience, and they occur in country and in town, and in the most different stages of education.

Yes, Mr. James, for the purpose of your immediate argument "this cluster of gifts may almost be said to constitute experience." But for our argument it does, and accurately, constitute imaginative genius. It is the gift that taught Xenophanes, watching the stars, to catch the whole piece from the pattern and cry out "All is one—" the gift that suddenly hitches the particular upon the universal and gives us a Falstaff, a Don Quixote, a Tartuffe, My Uncle Toby, the Vicar of Wakefield—

Forms more real than living man.

You know—you must know—that none of these is a photographic portrait of a living person—of a certain eccentric lodger whom Dickens had studied in Goswell Street, of a certain bibulous nurse resident in Kingsgate Street, High Holborn, "at a bird-fancier's, next door but one to the celebrated mutton-pie shop"—but children of imagination begotten upon it by some such observant moment as was vital to Mr. James's lady novelist. What, in fact, was the genesis of Mr. Pickwick? Dickens, you recall, was to write the letterpress accompaniment to a series of humorous sporting sketches by Seymour. The publisher Mr. Chapman, of Chapman and Hall, has left this uncontradicted record:

As this letter is to be historical, I may as well claim what little belongs to me in the matter, and that is the figure of Pickwick. Seymour's first sketch was of a long, thin man. The present immortal one he made from my description of a friend of mine at Richmond—a fat old beau who would wear, in spite of the ladies' protests, drab tights and black gaiters. His name was John Foster.[1]

Seymour drew the figure from Mr. Chapman's description: Dickens put life into it—yet more life—and made it a "nurseling of immortality." That, believe me, is how it happens; just so, and in no other way: and the operative power is called Genius. Remind yourselves of this when learned men, discussing Shakespeare, assure you they have fished the particular murex up which dyed Hamlet's inky cloak. Themselves are the cuttle, and only theirs is the ink.

II

But we talk of Dickens: and the trouble with Dickens is that he—whose brain in creating personage I suppose

[1] Is there not a blend of Mr. Tracy Tupman here?

to be the most fecund that ever employed itself on fiction—to the end of his days kept a curious distrust of himself and a propensity for this childish expedient of "drawing from the life." It is miserable, to me, to think of this giant who could turn off a Pickwick, a Sam Weller, a Dick Swiveller, a Mark Tapley, a Sarah Gamp, Captain Cuttle, Mr. Dick, Mr. Toots, Mr. Crummles, Mr. Mantalini, Dodson and Fogg, Codlin and Short, Spenlow and Jorkins, Mrs. Jellaby, Mrs. Billickin, Mrs. Gargery, Mrs. Wilfer, Mr. Twemlow, Mr. and Mrs. Micawber, Mr. Sapsea, Silas Wegg, and indeed anyone you take into your own experience of life—from Mr. Chadband to the Dolls' Dressmaker, with hundreds of lesser characters no less distinct—it is miserable to me, I say, that a Genius with all this largess to mint and scatter should have taxed his acquaintance to stamp their effigies upon poorer coin.

III

But let us discriminate. In "drawing from life" much will depend, as Aristotle might say, on (a) the extent, (b) the manner, (c) your intention: as likewise upon (d) the person drawn. I exclude all such portraits as are likely to provoke an action at law; for these come to be assessed under separate rules of criticism: and in general we may say of them that they should be avoided from the instinct of self-preservation rather than on grounds of disinterested aesthetic.

Confining ourselves, then, to portraits which are not actionable, we may take, as an extreme instance, Samuel Butler's *The Way of All Flesh*. For in this book the persons portrayed are the author's own parents, and he portrays them in a manner and with intention to make them odious, and to any extent: which seems to involve the nice moral question whether a person the best able to do a thing should not sometimes be the person who least ought to do it. And should the injunction against laying hands on your father Parmenides cover Parmenides if he happen to be your maiden aunt?—and maybe, too, she can retort, because you come of a literary family, you know! This power of retort, again, complicates a question which, you perceive, begins to be delicate. Ought you to catch anyone and hit him where he cannot hit back? Parmenides is no longer a relative but (say) a publisher, and you have—or think you have—reason to believe that he has cheated you. (And before you answer that this is incredible, let me say that I am dealing with an actual case, in which, however, I was not a party.) Are you justified in writing a work of fiction which holds him up to public opprobrium under a thin disguise? In my opinion you are not: because it means your attacking the fellow from a plane on which he can get no footing, to retaliate.

But it may be urged against him that Dickens by consent, and pretty well on his own admission, drew portraits of his mother in Mrs. Nickleby, and of his father in Mr. Micawber, and again in old Mr. Dorrit of the Marshalsea—this last, I am sure, the nearest to life. Well, I pass the question of provocation or moral excuse, observing only that Dickens tholed a childhood of culpable, even of damnable, neglect, whereas the parents of Samuel Butler did at least wing, with a Shrewsbury and Cambridge education, the barbs he was to shoot into their dead breasts. Dickens' parents turned him down, at ten, to a blacking-factory, and, as we saw in our last lecture, when the moment came

to release him from the blacking-warehouse his mother
tried to insist on his returning.

"I do not," he records to Forster, "write resentfully or
angrily, for I know how all these things have worked together to make me what I am; but I never afterwards
forgot, I never shall forget, I never can forget, that my
mother was warm for my being sent back."

IV

So there was provocation in plenty, humiliation
inflicted on a young and infinitely sensitive mind. But,
when we have granted that Dickens borrowed from
his mother for Mrs. Nickleby, from his father for Mr.
Micawber and the Elder Dorrit, mark you how genius
diverges from the mere hint—how far Micawber differs
from Dorrit, while both are elemental. Mark you
further how and while both are sublimated and Mrs.
Nickleby too—how much charity has to do with the
chemical process. Who thinks of Mrs. Nickleby but
as an amiable noodle? Who of Mr. Micawber, but to
enjoy his company? Who of Mr. Dorrit but with a
sad ironical pity? Where in any portrait of the three
can you trace a stroke of that vindictiveness you find
bitten upon page after page of *The Way of All Flesh*?
Moreover, choosing Old Dorrit, the least sympathetically but the most subtly drawn of the three, I
would ask you, studying that character for yourselves,
to note how Dickens conveys that, while much of its
infirmity is native, much also comes of the punishment
of the Marshalsea against which the poor creature's
pomposities are at once a narcotic, and a protest, however futile, of the dignity of a human soul, however
abject. Mark especially, at the close of Chapter

XXXV, how delicately he draws the shade of the
Marshalsea over Little Dorrit herself. He would fain
keep her, born and bred in that unwholesome den, its
one uncontaminated "prison-flower"—but with all his
charity he is (as I tried to show you in a previous
lecture) a magisterial artist and the truth compels him.
Mark then the workings of this child's mind on hearing
the glad news of her father's release. Here is the
passage:

Little Dorrit had been thinking too. After softly putting
his [her father's] hair aside, and touching his forehead
with her lips, she looked towards Arthur, who came nearer
to her, and pursued in a low whisper the subject of her
thoughts.

"Mr. Clennam, will he pay all his debts before he leaves
here?"

"No doubt. All."

"All the debts for which he has been imprisoned here,
all my life and longer?"

"No doubt."

There was something of uncertainty and remonstrance
in her look; something that was not all satisfaction. He
wondered to detect it, and said:

"You are glad that he should do so?"

"Are you?" asked Little Dorrit wistfully.

"Am I? Most heartily glad!"

"Then I know I ought to be."

"And are you not?"

"It seems to me hard," said Little Dorrit, "that he
should have lost so many years and suffered so much, and
at last pay all the debts as well. It seems to me hard that
he should pay in life and money both."

"My dear child——" Clennam was beginning.

"Yes, I know I am wrong," she pleaded timidly. "Don't
think any worse of me; it has all grown up with me here."

The prison, which could spoil so many things, had tainted Little Dorrit's mind no more than this. Engendered as the confusion was, in compassion for the poor prisoner, her father, it was the first speck Clennam had ever seen, it was the last speck Clennam ever saw, of the prison atmosphere upon her.

Now I call that, Gentlemen, the true novelist's stroke; rightly divined, so suddenly noted that we, who had not expected it, consent at once with a "Yes, yes—of course it happened so."

V

But what I wish you to grasp is—in a man who could play strokes like that by the score and conjure up out of his vasty deeps anything from Dick Swiveller to Uncle Pumblechook, from the Marchioness to Mrs. Joe Gargery—the silliness of diffidence which drove him again and again to mere copying "from the life." The superstition was idle, even when it did no harm. Having, in *Oliver Twist*, to describe a harsh and insolent Magistrate, Dickens (who could invent a Mr. Nupkins at will) took pains to be introduced to the Hatton Garden Police Court over which a certain Mr. Laing presided. He took these pains scrupulously, through an official channel (as they say), with the double result that we get Mr. Fang in the novel and that the Home Secretary very soon found it convenient to remove Mr. Laing from the Bench—and this, maybe, was all for the good—but you see how our author has already mixed up his conception of Charles Dickens as an author with that of Charles Dickens as a popular institution.

We will suppose that this Mr. Laing got his deserts.

None the less Dickens was hitting him on a pitch where he had no standing and could not hit back. And I would warn you of this, Gentlemen—that if, trained here, you go forth to do battle with wrongdoing, one of two methods is equally fair, and no other. Either you must persuade men generally that such and such a principle should govern their actions, or, if you have to take a particular wrongdoer by the throat, you should in the first place be absolutely sure of your facts, and, in the second, take him preferably on his own ground: so that his defeat will be righteous and plain to all, and he can excuse nothing on your advantage of position.

I have diverged into advising you as artists in public life: but the advice is not irrelevant, for it echoes that which, repeatedly given to Dickens by his best friends, he repeatedly ignored, yet never without detriment to his art and not seldom with irritating personal consequences. You all know how he came to grief over his caricatures of Landor and Leigh Hunt in *Bleak House*. Laurence Boythorne was merely a cheap superficial, not ill-natured, portrait. Landor, who never condescended to notice it, might well have shrugged his tall shoulders and said, "Is this the friend who visited Fiesole for my sake, and sent me home the only gift I demanded—an ivy-leaf from my old Villa there . . . and is *this* what he knows of me, or even what I seemed to him?" (The ivy-leaf was found wrapped away among Landor's papers, twenty years later.) But nothing—least of all its verisimilitude—can excuse the outrage perpetrated upon Leigh Hunt in the mask of Harold Skimpole: for, as Forster observes, to this character in the plot itself of *Bleak House* is assigned a part which no fascinating foibles or gaieties of speech could redeem from contempt. Hunt, who (with all his faults) never lacked generosity, had been among the first to hail and help Dickens, was (as often happens) the last to recognise himself for the intended victim: but when some kind friend drew his attention to the calculated wound, it went deep. Dickens apologised in a letter which did its best, but could, in the nature of things, amount to no more than kindly evasiveness. He was guilty, and he knew it. Hunt had been wounded in the house of his friend. It was all very well, or ill, for Dickens to plead (as he did) that in Micawber and Mrs. Nickleby he had played a like trick on his own father and mother. The first and most obvious answer to that is, "Well, if you did, you ought to have known better"—the second, "And, anyhow, why should that make it any the more agreeable to *me?*" But Mrs. Nickleby and Mr. Micawber (as we saw) are kindly, even lovable characters. Harold Skimpole is at once abject and mischievous: and as Forster very justly remarks:

The kindly or unkindly impression makes all the difference where liberties are taken with a friend; and even this entirely favourable condition will not excuse the practice to many, where near relatives are concerned.

But Landor and Leigh Hunt, you may say, were literary men of their hands, well able to defend themselves. Well, then, take down your *David Copperfield* and compare the Miss Mowcher of Chapter XXII with the Miss Mowcher of Chapter XXXII. You will see at once that something very queer has happened; that the Miss Mowcher of the earlier chapter, obviously meant to be an odious little go-between in the Steerforth plot, has changed into a decent little creature at once pathetic and purposeless. Why? The answer is that the deformed original, recognising her portrait, had in the interim addressed to Dickens a poignant letter of remonstrance. Dickens, writing the story in monthly numbers, apologised and hastily readjusted his plot.

These things work out to this—that in dealing with Dickens we have to lay our account—as in dealing with Shakespeare we have to lay our account—with a genius capable of vast surprises but at any point liable to bolt out of self-control. I have no theories at all of what a genius should be, or of how it ought to behave. Let us take what the gods give and be thankful: and with Dickens as with Shakespeare—both of whom write execrably at times and at times above admiration—we have to accept this inequality as a condition of our arriving at the very best. Even if we allow that a stricter schooling would have spoilt both, and is indeed the bane of originality: still let us keep our heads and tell ourselves that a great part of *Oliver Twist* is execrable stuff and no less, as the talk of Speed in *The Two Gentlemen of Verona* or of Lucio in *Measure for Measure* is execrable stuff and no less. By all means let us keep in mind that these flagrancies are human and, if you will, a necessary part of any Shakespeare, of any Dickens. But let us be quite clear in judging them as counterweights, and tell ourselves that a Virgil or a Dante—yes, or a Cervantes—would never need to ask such forgiveness from us.

VI

Corruptio optimi pessima is one of those orotund sayings which impress for the moment but are liable to ᵔ

have their wisdom very considerably spokeshaved (so
to speak) as soon as we apply the Socratic knife. Is
Tarzan of the Apes, after all, a corruption of the best?
And, if so, from what incalculable height did Lucifer
plunge, and how many days did he take before he broke
the roof of the railway station and scattered himself
over the bookstalls? We may derive solace, if we
will, by telling ourselves that those horrible days in
the Chandos Street blacking-warehouse were a part of
the education of Dickens' genius, taught it to *observe*,
and so on. But I say to you, as he said of Little Dorrit,
that such a shadow of cruelty, induced upon a sensitive
boy, must inevitably leave its stain: and I do most
earnestly ask you, some of whom may find yourselves
trustees for the education of poor children, if you are
sure that Dickens himself was the better for a starved
childhood? For my part I can give that starvation
little credit for his achievement, reading its effect
rather into his many faults of taste and judgment.

VII

It is usual to class among the first of these faults a
defective sense of English prose: and the commonest
arraignment lies against his use of blank verse in
moments of pathos or of deep emotion. Well, but let
us clear our minds of cant about English prose, and
abstain from talking about it as if the Almighty had
invented its final pattern somewhere in the eighteenth
century. Prose—and Poetry too, for that matter—
is a way of putting things worth record into memorable
speech. English writers of the late seventeenth and
the eighteenth century found, with some measure of
consent, an admirable fashion of doing this, and have

left a tradition: and it is a tradition to which I, personally, would cling if I could, admiring it as I do, and admiring so much less many pages of Dickens and a thousand of pages of Carlyle. After all, so long as the thing gets itself said, and effectively, and memorably, who are we to prescribe rules or parse sentences? What, for example, could that mysterious body, the College of Preceptors, do to improve the grammar of *Antony and Cleopatra*, even if they persuaded one another "Well, apparently they have come to stay, and perhaps we had better call upon them, my dear"?

VIII

Having, then, no preconceived notions about prose, and few prejudices save against certain locutions of which I confess I dislike them mainly because I dislike the sort of person who employs them—I assert that Dickens, aiming straight at his purpose, wrote countless pages of quite splendid prose. I defy you, for example, to suggest how a sense of the eeriness of the Woolwich marshes with an apprehension of horror behind the fog could be better conveyed in words than Dickens conveys them in the opening chapters of *Great Expectations*; as I ask you how the earliest impressions of a sensitive child can be better conveyed in language than they are in the early chapters of *David Copperfield*.

IX

But even this apologia—sufficient as I think it—does not cover the whole defence. We have picked up a habit of consenting with critics who tell us that Dickens' prose is careless and therefore not worth studying. Believe me, you are mistaken if you believe these critics. Dickens sometimes wrote execrably: far oftener he penned at a stretch page upon page of comment and conversation that brilliantly effect their purpose and are, *therefore*, good writing. You will allow, I dare say, his expertness in glorifying the loquacity that comes of a well-meaning heart and a rambling head. Recall, for example—casually chosen out of hundreds—Mrs. Chivery on her son John, nursing his love-lornness amid the washing in the back-yard: and remark the *idiom* of it:

"It's the only change he takes," said Mrs. Chivery, shaking her head afresh. "He won't go out, even to the back-yard, when there's no linen: but when there's linen to keep the neighbours' eyes off, he'll sit there, hours. Hours he will. Says he feels as if it was groves. . . . Our John has everyone's good word and everyone's good wish. He played with her as a child when in that yard she played. He has known her ever since. He went out upon the Sunday afternoon when in this very parlour he had dined, and met her, with appointment or without appointment which I do not pretend to say. He made his offer to her. Her brother and sister is high in their views and against Our John. 'No, John, I cannot have you, I cannot have any husband, it is not my intentions ever to become a wife, it is my intentions to be always a sacrifice, farewell. Find another worthy of you and forget me!' This is the way in which she is doomed to be a constant slave, to them that are not worthy that a constant slave unto them she should be. This is the way in which Our John has come to find no pleasure but in taking cold among the linen. . . ."

Is *that* not prose? Of course it is prose *for its purpose*: and, strictly for her purpose—strictly, mind you

for their purpose—Mrs. Chivery's parallelisms of speech
will match those of the prophet Jeremiah at his literary
best. "Ah," say you, "but Dickens is dealing out
humorous reported speech. Can he write prose of his
own?" Well, yes, and yes most certainly. If you
will search and study his passages of deliberate writing
you will scarcely miss to see how he derives in turn of
phrase as in intonation from the great eighteenth-
century novelists and translators whose works, if you
remember, were the small child's library in the beautiful fourth chapter of *David Copperfield*:

> My father had left a small collection of books in a little
> room upstairs . . . which nobody else in our house ever
> troubled. From that blessed little room, Roderick Ran-
> dom, Peregrine Pickle, Humphrey Clinker, Tom Jones, the
> Vicar of Wakefield, Don Quixote, Gil Blas, and Robinson
> Crusoe came out, a glorious host, to keep me company. . . .

The whole passage, if you will turn to it, you will
recognise as delicate English prose. But it is also a
faithful, if translated, record. From this line of
English writers, the more you study him, the more
clearly you will recognise Dickens as standing in the
direct descent of a pupil. He brings something of his
own, of course, to infuse it, as genius will: and that
something is usually a hint of pathos which the eight-
eenth-century man avoided. But (this touch of
pathos excepted) you will find little, say, to distinguish
Fielding's sketch of Squire Allworthy on his morning
stroll from this sketch, which I take casually from *The
Old Curiosity Shop*, of an aged woman punctually
visiting the grave of her husband who had died in his
prime of twenty-three:

"Yes, I was his wife. Death doesn't change no more than life, my dear." . . . And now that five-and-fifty years were gone, she spoke of the dead man as if he had been her son or grandson, with a kind of pity for his youth growing out of her own old age, and an exalting of his strength and manly beauty, as compared with her own weakness and decay; and yet she spoke of him as her husband too, and thinking of herself in connection with him, as she used to be and not as she was now, talked of their meeting in another world, as if he were dead but yesterday, and she, separated from her former self, were thinking of the happiness of that comely girl who seemed to have died with him.

X

No, we can none of us afford to despise Dickens' prose. This passage comes from one of his earliest books: if you would learn how he (ever a learner) learned to consolidate his style, study that neglected work of his, *The Uncommercial Traveller*—study such essays as that on "Wapping Workhouse" or that on "The City Churchyards"—study them with Thackeray's *Roundabout Papers*—and tell me if these two great Victorian novelists, after shaking the dust of an *Esmond* or a *David Copperfield* off their palms, cannot, as a parergon, match your Augustans—your Steele or your Addison— on their own ground. Few recognise it, this pair being otherwise so great: but it is so.

And because you will probably disbelieve me at first going-off, I shall add the testimony of one you will be apter to trust—that of George Gissing. I have spoken of one chapter in *David Copperfield*, to commend it.

But, says Gissing:

In the story of David Copperfield's journey on the Dover road we have as good a piece of narrative prose as can be found in English. Equally good, in another way, are those passages of rapid retrospect in which David tells us of his later boyhood, a concentration of memory perfumed with the sweetest humour. It is not an easy thing to relate, with perfect proportion of detail, with interest that never for a moment drops, the course of a year or two of wholly uneventful marriage: but read the chapter entitled *Our Domestic Life* and try to award adequate praise to the great artist who composed it. One can readily suggest how the chapter could have been spoiled; ever so little undue satire, ever so little excess of sentiment; but who can point to a line in which it might be bettered? It is perfect writing: one can say no more and no less.

XI

I am glad, Gentlemen, on the verge of concluding these talks about Dickens, to quote this from Gissing—a genuine genius, himself an author of what Dr. Johnson would have described as "inspissated gloom." There is, I daresay, some heaven of recognition in which all true artists meet; and at any rate it pleases one to think that the author of *The New Grub Street* should, in this sublunary sphere, have been comforted on his way (it would even seem, entranced) by such children of joy as Sam Weller and Mr. Toots. And I, at any rate, who admired Gissing in life, like to think of him who found this world so hard, now, by virtue of his love for Dickens, reconciled to look down on it from that other sphere, with tolerant laughter—upon this queer individual England, at least. For Providence has made and kept this nation a comfortable nation, even to this day: and if you take its raciest literature from Chaucer down, you may assure yourselves that much of its glorious merit rests on the "triple pillar" of common-sense, religious morality and hearty laughter. I for my part hold that we shall help a great deal to restore our commonwealth by seeking back to that last "Godlike function" and re-learning it. To promote that laughter, with good sense and good morality, was ever Dickens' way, as to kill wherever he could what he once called "this custom of putting the natural demand for amusement out of sight, as some untidy housekeepers put dust, and pretending that it was swept away." And I think of Dickens as a great Englishman not least in this, that he was a man of his hands, with a great laugh scattering humbug to make place for mirth and good-will; "a clean hearth and [to adapt Mrs. Battle] the *spirit* of the game."

XII

I conclude these lectures on Dickens with a word or two casually uttered in conversation by a great man —possibly the greatest—of the generation that succeeded Dickens; himself a superb novelist, and a ruthless thinker for the good of his kind; a Russian, moreover, to whom the language alone of Sam Weller or of Mrs. Gamp must have presented difficulties wellnigh inconceivable by us. Some nineteen years ago a friend of mine visited Tolstoy at his home and, the talk falling upon Dickens, this is what Tolstoy said:

All his characters are my personal friends. I am constantly comparing them with living persons, and living persons with them. And what a *spirit* there was in all he wrote!

This having been reported to Swinburne, here is a part of Swinburne's answer:

What a superb and crushing reply to the vulgar insults of such malignant boobies and poetasters as G. H. Lewes and Co. (too numerous a Co.!) is the witness of . . . such a man among men! . . . After all, like will to like— genius will find out genius, and goodness will recognise goodness.

Tolstoy to Dickens. . . . *That* is how the tall ships, the grandees of literature, dip their flags and salute as they pass. Gentlemen, let us leave it at that!

THACKERAY (I)

I

AMONG many wise sayings left behind him by
the late Sir Walter Raleigh—*our* Sir Walter and
Oxford's of whom his pupils there would say, "But
Raleigh is a prince"—there haunts me as I begin to
speak of Thackeray, a slow remark dropped as from an
afterthought upon those combatants who are for ever
extorting details of Shakespeare's private life out of the
Plays and the Sonnets, and those others (Browning, for
example, and Matthew Arnold) who in revulsion have
preached Shakespeare up for the grand impersonal
artist who never unlocked his heart, who smiles down
upon all questioning and is still

> Out-topping knowledge.

Such a counter-claim may be plausible—is at any rate
excusable if only as an oath upon the swarm of pedlars
who infest Shakespeare and traffic in obscure hints of
scandal. Yet, it will not work. "It would never be
entertained," says Raleigh, "by an artist, and would
have had short shrift from any of the company that
assembled at the Mermaid Tavern. No man can
walk abroad save on his own shadow. No dramatist
can create live characters save by bequeathing the best
of himself to the children of his art, scattering among

them a largess of his own qualities, giving, it may be, to one his wit, to another his philosophic doubt, to another his love of action, to another the simplicity and constancy that he finds deep in his own nature. There is no thrill of feeling communicated from the printed page but has first been alive in the mind of the author: there was nothing alive in his mind that was not intensely and sincerely felt. Plays like Shakespeare's cannot be written in cold blood; they call forth the man's whole energies, and take toll of the last farthing of his wealth of sympathy and experience."

II

No man can walk abroad save on his own shadow. That is the sentence, of truly Johnsonian common-sense, which bears most intimately on our subject this morning. The story runs that Thackeray, one day tapping impatiently upon the cover of some adulatory memoir of somebody, warm from the press, enjoined upon his family, "None of this nonsense about me, after my death": and the injunction was construed by his daughter, Lady Ritchie, most piously beyond a doubt, perhaps too strictly, for certain not with the happiest results. For this denial of any authoritative biography—of a writer and a clean-living English gentleman who might, if any human being can or could, have walked up to the Recording Angel and claimed his *dossier* without a blush—has not only let in a flood of spurious reminiscences, anecdotes, sayings he most likely never uttered or at least never uttered with meaning or accent to give pain that, as reported, they convey. It has led to a number of editions with gossipy prefaces and filial chat (I fear I must say it) none the more helpful for being tinctured by affection and qualified by reserve.

This happens to be the more unfortunate of Thackeray since, as I suppose, no writer of the Victorian age walked abroad more sturdily on his own tall shadow, or trusted more on it. It was a shadow, too: dark enough for any man's footstep. I do not wish— nor is it necessary—to break in upon any reticence. But you probably know the main outline of the story— of a Cambridge youth, of Trinity, who living moderately beyond his means (as undergraduates will) lost his affluence, lost the remains of it when, bolting to London, he dared to run a newspaper—two newspapers. *The National Standard* had soon (in his own phrase) to be hauled down, and *The Constitutional* belied its title by a rapid decline and decease. Thus he lost a moderate patrimony, and we find him next as a roving journalist in Paris, divided between pen and pencil, with an almost empty pocket. There, in August, 1836, at the British Embassy, he made a most imprudent but happy marriage—most happy, that is for a while. Years afterwards he wrote to a young friend:

I married at your age with £400 paid by a newspaper which failed six months afterwards, and always love to hear of a young man testing his fortune in that way. Though my marriage was a wreck, as you know, I would do it over again, for behold Love is the crown and completion of all earthly good. . . . The very best and pleasantest house I ever knew in my life had but £300 to keep it.

Here, then, comes in the tragedy of Thackeray's life. Daughters were born to him amid those pleasures and anxieties which only they can taste fully who earn their

daily bread in mutual love on the future's chance. As
he beautifully wrote, long after, in *Philip:*

I hope, friend, you and I are not too proud to ask for
our daily bread, and to be grateful for getting it? Mr.
Philip had to work for his, in care and trouble, like other
children of men:—to work for it, and I hope to pray for it
too. It is a thought to me awful and beautiful, that of
the daily prayer, and of the myriads of fellow-men utter-
ing it, in care and in sickness, in doubt and in poverty, in
health and in wealth. *Panem nostrum da nobis hodie.*
Philip whispers it by the bedside where wife and child lie
sleeping, and goes to his early labour with a stouter heart:
as he creeps to his rest when the day's labour is over, and
the quotidian bread is earned, and breathes his hushed
thanks to the bountiful Giver of the meal. All over this
world what an endless chorus is singing of love, and thanks,
and prayer. Day tells to day the wondrous story, and
night recounts it unto night. How do I come to think of a
sunrise which I saw near twenty years ago on the Nile
when the river and sky flushed with the dawning light and,
as the luminary appeared, the boatmen knelt on the rosey
deck and adored Allah? So, as thy sun rises, friend, over
the humble housetops round about your home, shall you
wake many and many a day to duty and labour. May
the task have been honestly done when the night comes;
and the steward deal kindly with the labourer.

Always this refrain in Thackeray—the text which
Dr. Johnson once had inscribed on his watch, *ΝΥΞ ΓΑΡ
ΕΡΧΕΤΑΙ,* "For the night cometh."

With the birth of her third child, however, Mrs.
Thackeray fell under a mental disease not violent at
first, but deepening until it imperatively required
removal and restraint.

III

I have been as short over this as could be: but the simple fact must be taken into account if we would understand Thackeray at all. Without knowledge of it, for instance, how can we interpret the ache behind his jolly *Ballad of Bouillabaisse?*

> This Bouillabaisse a noble dish is—
> A sort of soup, or broth, or brew,
> Or hotchpotch, of all sorts of fishes,
> That Greenwich never could outdo;
> Green herbs, red peppers, mussels, saffern,
> Soles, onions, garlic, roach, and dace;
> All these you eat at Terré's tavern,
> In that one dish of Bouillabaisse . . .
>
> Ah me! how quick the days are flitting!
> I mind me of a day that's gone,
> When here I'd sit, as now I'm sitting,
> In this same place—but not alone.
> A fair young form was nestled near me,
> A dear, dear face looked fondly up,
> And sweetly spoke and smiled to cheer me
> —There's no one now to share my cup.

If you wish, taking him at his best, to envisage Thackeray in the days of his assured triumph, you must understand him as a desolated man; as a man who, having built a fine house for himself in Kensington Palace Gardens, could never fit it for a real home. If he built himself a house, he could not sit and write in it; scarcely a page of *The Newcomes* was written but on Club paper or at a hotel. It would seem as if the very anguish of the hearth drove this soul, so domestic by instinct, into the waste of Clubland, Pall Mall, the Reform Club, where his portrait now so pathetically hangs. For above all (let *The Rose and the Ring* with its delightful and delicate occasion attest) Thackeray was born to be beloved of a nursery—the sort of great fellow to whom on entrance every child, as every dog, takes by instinct. In the nursery, quite at home, he rattles off the gayest unforgettable verses:

> Did you ever hear of Miss Symons?
> She lives at a two-penny pieman's:
> > But when she goes out
> > To a ball or a rout
> Her stomacher's all covered with di'monds.

Or, for elder taste,

> In the romantic little town of Highbury,
> My father kept a Succulating Libary.
> He followed in his youth the Man immortal who
> Conquered the Frenchman on the plains of Waterloo

—with similar fooling. Some men at Cambridge had the gift of this fooling—in Tennyson's day, too—and not the least of them was Edward Lear, incomparable melodist of nonsense—nursery Mozart of the Magic Flute—to whom, on his Travels in Greece, Tennyson dedicated those very lovely stanzas beginning:

> Illyrian woodlands, echoing falls
> > Of water, sheets of summer glass,
> > The long divine Peneian pass,
> The vast Acroceraunian walls . . .

He must be an unsympathetic critic (I think) and therefore an incomplete critic, if indeed a critic at all,

who feels any real incongruity as in his mind he lets
those lines fade off into

> Far and few, far and few,
> Are the lands where the Jumblies live, etc.;

for as Shelley once assured us, more or less:

> Many a green isle needs must be
> In the deep wide sea of—Philistie,

and to anyone who remembers the imaginary horizons
of his nursery I dare say the Blessed Isles of Nonsense
and the land where the Bong tree grows lie not far from
Calypso's grot, or the house of Circe

> In gardens near the pale of Proserpine,
> Where that Æaean isle forgets the main . . .

or the yellow sands of Prospero's island where the
elves curtsy, kiss and dance, or Sindbad's cave, or those
others "measureless to man" rushed through by Alph
the sacred river to where we

> see the children sport upon the shore,
> And hear the mighty waters rolling evermore.

IV

No: I am not talking fantastically at all. Let us be
sober-serious, corrugating our brows upon history:
and at once see that these Cambridge men of Thackeray's generation—FitzGerald (to whom he was "old
Thack"), Tennyson, Brookfield, Monckton Milnes,

Kinglake—all with the exception of Arthur Hallam
(whom I sadly suspect to have been something of a
prig) cultivated high fooling and carried it to the *n*th
power as a fine art. Life, in that Victorian era of peace
between wars, was no lull of lotus eating for them—
the England of Carlyle, Newman, Ruskin admitted no
lull of the young mind—but a high-spirited hilarious
game. As one of them, Milnes, wrote of "The Men
of Old":

> They went about their gravest deeds
> As noble boys at play.

A plenty of English writers—some of them accounted
highly serious writers—had indulged in what I may call
similar "larks" before them. Swift, for example, has a
glorious sense of the high-nonsensical; Cowper has it,
of course. I regret to say that I even suspect Crabbe.
Canning had it—take, for example, a single stage-
direction in *The Rovers:*

> Several soldiers cross the stage wearily, as if returning
> from the Thirty Years' War.

Lamb of course had it; and in his letters will carry it
to a *delirium in excelsis*. But this Cambridge group
would seem to have shared and practised it as a form,
an exercise, in their free-masonry. Take for a single
instance James Spedding's forehead. James Spedding,
afterwards learned editor of Bacon, and a butt in that
profane set, had a brow severe and high, of the sort
(you know) that tells of moral virtue with just a hint
of premature baldness. It was very smooth; it rose
to a scalp all but conical. His admiring friends elected

to call it Alpine.   Now hear FitzGerald upon it, in a letter:

That portrait of Spedding, for instance, which Lawrence has given me: not swords, nor cannon, nor all the Bulls of Bashan butting at it, could, I feel sure, discompose that venerable forehead.   No wonder that no hair can grow at such an altitude: no wonder his view of Bacon's virtue is so rarefied that the common consciences of men cannot endure it.   Thackeray and I occasionally amuse ourselves with the idea of Spedding's forehead: we find it somehow or other in all things, just peering out of all things: you see it in a milestone, Thackeray says.   He also draws the forehead rising with a sober light over Mont Blanc, and reflected in the lake of Geneva.   The forehead is at present in Pembrokeshire, I believe: or Glamorganshire: or Monmouthshire: it is hard to say which.   It has gone to spend its Christmas there.

And later, May 22, 1842:

You have of course read the account of Spedding's forehead landing in America.   English sailors hail it in the Channel, mistaking it for Beachy Head.

I have quoted this just to enforce my argument that, to understand Thackeray's work, you must understand just what kind of a man he was in his upbringing and the way of his early friendships.   And when I add that his gift for nursery folly was expended upon a widowed and desolate home—on a home from which his heart drove him to flee, no matter how ambitiously he rebuilt and adorned it, to scribble his novels on Club paper or in hotels, you may get (I hope) a little closer to understanding his generous, but bitter and always sad heart.

V

I must dwell on another point, too. The Thackerays (or Thackwras—which I suppose to be another form of Dockwras) had for some generations prospered and multiplied as Anglo-Indians in the service of the old East India Company. Their tombs are thick in the old graveyard of Calcutta, and I would refer anyone who would ponder their epitaphs, or is interested in the stock from which Thackeray sprang, to a little book by the late Sir William Hunter entitled *The Thackerays in India and some Calcutta Graves* (Henry Frowde, London: 1897). Thackeray himself was born at Calcutta on the 18th of July, 1811, and, according to the sad fate of Anglo-Indian children, was shipped home to England at the age of five, just as Clive Newcome is shipped home in the novel; and when he pictured the sad figure of Colonel Newcome tottering back up the *ghaut*, or river-stairs, Thackeray drew what his own boyish eyes had seen and his small heart suffered. Turn to the "Roundabout Paper" *On Letts's Diary* and you will read concerning that parting:

I wrote this, remembering in long, long distant days, such a *ghaut*, or river-stair, at Calcutta, and a day when down those steps, to a boat which was in waiting, came two children, whose mothers remained on the shore. One of those ladies was never to see her boy more. . . . We were first cousins; had been little playmates and friends from the time of our birth; and the first house in London to which I was taken was that of our aunt, the mother of his Honour the Member of Council.

This young cousin and playmate returned in time, as Thackeray never did, to the shore they were leaving;

and died Sir Richmond Shakespeare (no *vile nomen!*),
Agent to the Governor-General for Central India. The
news of his death gave occasion to the tender little
essay from which I have been quoting.

On the passage their ship touched at St. Helena, and
their black servant took them a long walk over rocks
and hills "until we reached a garden, where we saw a
man walking. 'That's he,' said the black man: 'that
is Bonaparte! He eats three sheep every day, and all
the little children he can lay hands upon.'"—After
which terrible vision no doubt the youngsters resumed
their Odyssey—as Homer would put it—

$$\text{ἀκαχήμενοι ἦτορ,}$$
$$\text{ἄσμενοι ἐκ θανάτοιο.}$$

"Stricken at heart yet rejoicing to have escaped per-
dition." They reached London to find it plunged in
mourning (and, for many reasons, in very genuine
mourning) by the death of the Princess Charlotte: and
young Thackeray proceeded to Chiswick, to the charge
and care of his aunt Mrs. Ritchie. One day she caught
the child trying on his uncle's large hat, and, finding
to her alarm that it accurately fitted him, swept him off
to the fashionable physician, Sir Charles Clark: "Reassure yourself, madam," the doctor is reported as saying: "he has, to be sure, an abnormal head; but I think
there's something in it." He was put to school first at
a young gentlemen's academy at Chiswick, maybe next
door to Miss Pinkerton's Seminary for Young Ladies
through the portals of which (if you remember, and into
the garden) Miss Rebecca Sharp hurled back her
"leaving copy" of Dr. Johnson's "Dixonary." The
master would seem to have been a Dr. Swishtail, com-

pounded of negligence and tyranny, as so many "private schoolmasters" chose to be even to days of my own experience. But here is the child's first letter, dated February 18, 1818, to his mother in India and composed in a round hand between ruled lines:

My dear Mama—I hope you are quite well. I have given my dear Grandmama a kiss. My aunt Ritchie is very good to me. I like Chiswick, there are so many good boys to play with. St. James's Park is a very nice place. St. Paul's Church, too, I like very much. It is a finer place than I expected. I hope Captain Smyth is well: Give my love to him and tell him he must bring you home to your affectionate little son.

WILLIAM THACKERAY.

The separating sea was wide: but what a plucky little letter!

VI

I shall lay stress on it for a moment because, as it seems to me, if we read between the childish lines, they not only evince the pluck of the child, and not only breathe a waft of the infinite pathos of English children, Indian born: but because I hold that no one who would understand Thackeray can afford to forget that he was of Anglo-Indian stock, bone and marrow.

Now I want, avoiding so much of offence as I may, to say a word or two (and these only as a groping through private experience, to illustrate Thackeray) about the retired Anglo-Indian as he has come within the range of a long experience at an English town by the seashore. On the whole I know of no human being

more typically pathetic. His retirement may be
happier in some places such as Cheltenham, where he
has a Club in which he can meet old Indian cronies or
men from "the other side," and tell stories and discuss
the only politics which interest them. But in any odd
angle of this capital yet most insular isle his isolation is
horrible and fatal. Compared with it, the sorrows of
a British child "sent home" (as conveyed, and to the
very heart, in Mr. Kipling's *Wee Willie Winkie*, for
example) are tragically insignificant. Youth is elastic
and can recover. But this grown man, through the
"long, long Indian days," has toiled and supported
himself upon a hope, to end in England with fishing or
shooting and a share of that happy hospitality which
(God knows) he has earned.

What happens? The domestic servant question
(always with us), cold rooms, dinner-parties at which
stories about Allahabad are listened to patiently by
ladies who confuse it with Lahore, polite men who
suggest a game of "snooker pool" as a relief, hoping for
not too many anecdotes in the course of it. And for
this your friend and his admirable wife have been nursing, feeding themselves on promise for, maybe, thirty
years and more, all the time and day after day—*there*
lies the tragedy—dutifully giving all their best, for
England, in confidence of its reward.

It is not altogether our fault. It is certainly not our
fault that the partridges do not rise on the stubble or
the salmon leap up and over the dams in such numbers
as the repatriated fondly remember. To advise a lady
accustomed to many Indian servants upon tact with a
couple or three of English ones—post-War too—is (as
Sir Thomas Browne might say) to bid her sleep in
Epicurus his faith, and reacclimatise her notion. But,

to be short, they talk to us politics which have no basis discoverable in this country.

Yet, withal, they are so noble! So simple in dignity! Far astray from any path of progress as we may think him; insane as we may deem his demand to rule, unreasonable his lament over the lost England of his youth which for so long he has sentimentalised, or domestic his interest in his nephews, the Anglo-Indian has that key of salvation which is loyalty. He is for England: and for that single cause I suppose no men or women that ever lived and suffered on earth have suffered more than those who lie now under the huddled gravestones of Calcutta.

VII

I am coming to this: that those who accuse Thackeray of being a snob (even under his own definition) should in fairness lay their account that he came of people who, commanding many servants, supported the English tradition of rule and dominance in a foreign land.

I believe this to explain him in greater measure than he has generally been explained or understood. Into a class so limited, so exiled, so professional in its aims and interests—so *borné* and repugnant against ideas that would invade upon the tried order of things and upset caste along with routine—so loyal to its own tradition of service, so dependent for all reward upon official recognition (which often means the personal caprice of some Governor or Secretary of State or Head of Department), some Snobbery—as we understand the word nowadays—will pretty certainly creep; to make its presence felt, if not to pervade. But I am not going to discuss with you the question, "Was Thackeray that thing he spent so much pains, such excessive pains, in denouncing?''—over which so many disputants have lost their tempers. It is not worth our while, as the whole business, to my thinking, was not worth Thackeray's while. When we come to it—as we must, because it bulks so largely in his work—we shall quickly pass on.

To me it seems that Thackeray's geniture and early upbringing—all those first impressions indelible in any artist—affected him in subtler ways far better worth our considering. Let me just indicate two.

VIII

For the first.—It seems to me that Thackeray—a social delineator or nothing—never quite understood the roots of English life or of the classes he chose to depict; those roots which even in Pall Mall or Piccadilly or the Houses of Parliament ramify underground deep and out, fetching their vital sap from the countryside. Walter Bagehot, after quoting from *Venus and Adonis* Shakespeare's famous lines on a driven hare, observes that "it is absurd to say we know *nothing* about the man who wrote that: we know he had been after a hare." I cannot find evidence in his works that this child, brought from Calcutta to Chiswick, transferred to the Charterhouse (then by Smithfield), to Cambridge, Paris, Fleet Street, Club-land, had ever been after a hare: and if you object that this means nothing, I retort that it means a great deal: it means that he never "got off the pavement." It means that he is on sure ground when he writes of Jos. Sedley, demi-nabob, but on no sure ground at all when he gets down to Queen's Crawley: that in depicting a class—now perhaps vanishing—he never, for example, got near the spirit that breathes in **Archdeacon Grantly's** talk with his gamekeeper:

"I do think, I do indeed, sir, that Mr. Thorne's man ain't dealing fairly along of the foxes. I wouldn't say a word about it, only that Mr. Henry is so particular."

"What about the foxes? What is he doing with the foxes?"

"Well, sir, he's a trapping on 'em. He is, indeed, your reverence. I wouldn't speak if I warn't well nigh mortial sure."

Now the archdeacon had never been a hunting man, though in his early days many a clergyman had been in the habit of hunting without losing his clerical character by doing so; but he had lived all his life among gentlemen in a hunting county, and had his own very strong ideas about the trapping of foxes. Foxes first, and pheasants afterwards, had always been the rule with him as to any land of which he himself had had the management. . . . But now his heart was not with the foxes,—and especially not with the foxes on behalf of his son Henry. "I can't have any meddling with Mr. Thorne," he said; "I can't and I won't . . . I'm sure he wouldn't have the foxes trapped."

"Not if he knowed it, he wouldn't, your reverence. A gentleman of the likes of him, who's been a hunting over fifty year, wouldn't do the likes of that; but the foxes is trapped . . . a vixen was trapped just across the field yonder, in Goshall Springs, no later than yesterday morning." Flurry was now thoroughly in earnest; and, indeed, the trapping of a vixen in February is a serious thing.

"Goshall Springs don't belong to me," said the archdeacon.

"No, your reverence; they're on the Ullathorne property. But a word from your reverence would do it. Mr. Henry thinks more of the foxes than anything. The last word he told me was that it would break his heart if he saw the coppices drawn blank. . . ."

"I will have no meddling in the matter, Flurry. . . . I will not have a word said to annoy Mr. Thorne." Then he rode away. . . .

But the archdeacon went on thinking, thinking, thinking. He could have heard nothing of his son to stir him more in his favour than this strong evidence of his partiality for foxes. I do not mean it to be understood that the archdeacon regarded foxes as better than active charity, or a contented mind, or a meek spirit, or than self-denying temperance. No doubt all these virtues did hold in his mind their proper places, altogether beyond contamination of foxes. But he had prided himself on thinking that his son should be a country gentleman. . . . On the same morning the archdeacon wrote the following note:—

DEAR THORNE,—My man tells me that foxes have been trapped on Darvell's farm, just outside the coppices. I know nothing of it myself, but I am sure you'll look to it.—
                              Yours always,
                                        T. GRANTLY.

Absurd? Very well—but you will never understand the politics of the last century—that era so absurdly viewed out of focus, just now, as one of mere industrial expansion—unless you lay your account with it better than Thackeray did. As you know, he once stood for Parliament, as Liberal candidate for the City of Oxford: and it is customary to rejoice over his defeat as releasing from party what was meant for mankind. In fact he never had a true notion of politics or of that very deep thing, political England. Compare his sense of it— his *novelist's* sense—with Disraeli's. He and Disraeli, as it happens, both chose to put the famous-infamous

Marquis of Hertford into a novel. But what a thing of cardboard, how entirely without atmosphere of political or social import, is Lord Steyne in *Vanity Fair* as against Lord Monmouth in *Coningsby!*

IX

The late Herman Merivale, in a very brilliant study, interrupted by death and left to be completed by Sir Frank Marzials, finds the two key-secrets (as he calls them) of Thackeray's life to be these—Disappointment and Religion. I propose ten days hence to examine this, and to speak of both. But I may premise, here and at once, that Thackeray was a brave man who took the knocks of life without flinching (even that from young Venables' fist, which broke his nose but not their friendship), and that to me the melancholy which runs through all his writing—the melancholy of Ecclesiastes, the eternal Mataiotes Mataioteton— Vanity of Vanities, all is Vanity—was drawn by origin from the weary shore of Ganges and brought in the child's blood to us, over the sea.

"Vanity of vanities," saith the Preacher—Thackeray was before all else a Preacher: and that is the end of it, whether in a set of Cornhill verses or in his most musical, most solemn, prose—

> How spake of old the Royal Seer?
> (His text is one I love to treat on.)
> This life of ours, he said, is sheer
>   Mataiotes Mataioteton . . . , etc.

And now hear the burden of it on that famous page telling how Harry Esmond walked home after breaking the news of Duke Hamilton's duel and death:

As Esmond and the Dean walked away from Kensington discoursing of this tragedy, and how fatal it was to the cause which they both had at heart, the street-criers were already out with their broadsides, shouting through the town the full, true, and horrible account of the death of Lord Mohun and Duke Hamilton in a duel. A fellow had got to Kensington, and was crying it in the square there at very early morning, when Mr. Esmond happened to pass by. He drove the man from under Beatrix's very window, whereof the casement had been set open. The sun was shining, though 'twas November: he had seen the market-carts rolling into London, the guard relieved at the palace, the labourers trudging to their work in the gardens between Kensington and the City—the wandering merchants and hawkers filling the air with their cries. The world was going to its business again, although dukes lay dead and ladies mourned for them, and kings, very likely, lost their chances. So night and day pass away, and to-morrow comes, and our place knows us not. Esmond thought of the courier now galloping on the North road, to inform him who was Earl of Arran yesterday that he was Duke of Hamilton to-day; and of a thousand great schemes, hopes, ambitions, that were alive in the gallant heart, beating a few hours since, and now in a little dust quiescent.

A heavy passage, Gentlemen—and commonplace? Ah! as you grow older you will find that most of the loveliest, most of the most sacred passages in literature are commonplaces exquisitely turned and tuned to catch and hold new hearts.

THACKERAY (II)

I

I LEFT off, Gentlemen, upon a saying of Herman Merivale's that the two key-secrets of Thackeray's life were Disappointment and Religion, and I proposed, examining this to-day, to speak of both.

Well, for the first, I have already (I think) given full room in the account to that domestic sorrow which drove him, great boon favourite of the nursery, to flee from his grand new house in Kensington Gardens—

> Cedes coemptis saltibus et domo
> Villaque—

to write his novels anywhere rather than at home. In the words of Barnes' beautiful lament, which I here make free to divorce from its native dialect—

> Since now beside my dinner-board
> Your voice does never sound,
> I'll eat the bit I can afford
> Afield upon the ground;
> Below the darksome bough, my love,
> Where you did never dine,
> And I don't grieve to miss you now
> As I at home do pine.

II

But those who stress this Disappointment in Thackeray go on to allege other causes, additional causes, for it: as that he lost a comfortable patrimony early in life, and that, conscious of great powers, he felt them for many years unappreciated, and, when appreciated, partially eclipsed by the popularity of his great rival, Dickens. Now I don't deny that one disappointment may accumulate upon another on a man: but I ask you to consider also that in criticism one nail may drive out another, and that in ordinary one explanation is better than two, almost always far better than three: the possible conclusion being that not one of the three—not even the first—is the right one.

Actually, then, Thackeray as a young man lost his patrimony by flinging the hazard quite gallantly and honourably, as a young man should; foolishly perhaps, as a young man will, but having been just as young and foolish I am even now not turned Cato enough to condemn a boy for that.   Let us see just what happened.

From the Charterhouse he came up here, to Trinity. His means have been variously computed: but you may put it down pretty safely at £500 a year—a very pretty sum indeed for an undergraduate.   What he did with it you may find for yourselves in those brilliant chapters in *Pendennis*—perhaps the very best written on University life—which treat of Pen's career at Cambridge.

(For it is Cambridge, of course, though he calls it Oxbridge.   And here may I parenthetically drop a long-hoarded curse upon that trick of the Victorian novelists of sending up their young heroes to Oxbridge or Camford, entering them usually at the College of St. Boniface, head of the river or just about to be head.

If, from the pages of Victorian fiction, a crew could be mustered to unmoor and paddle down the dear old 'Varsity barge, in the early June twilight, past the Pike and Eel to Iffley, there to await the crack of the rifle that loosens the tense muscles,—heavens! what a crew!—or, as Matthew Arnold would say, "what a set!"—all so indifferent to the rules of training, so like in appearance to young Greek gods, so thirsty!—and, on the run of it, what laurels for dear old St. Boniface! . . . I don't know why these hermaphrodite names "Oxbridge" and "Camford" have always been so peculiarly repugnant to me: but they always have been, and are. I feel somehow as if to be a graduate of either were to offend against the Table of Forbidden Degrees. But Thackeray achieved one success in the blending—when he combined "scout" and "gyp" into "skip.")

Oxbridge, then, in *Pendennis* is Cambridge. Thackeray came up in February, 1829—in the Lent term, that is, instead of in the previous October—I cannot discover for what reason. It made him, however, by the rules then prevailing, a *non ens* or *non annus* man for that year: and being also a non-reading man, he decided after two years of genially unprofitable residence, to refuse the Tripos and a degree, and retire on London, and took chambers at Hare Court in the Temple. His age was twenty.

III

Sainte-Beuve—I have read reasonably in his voluminous works, but without as yet happening on the passage which, quoted by Stevenson in his *Apology for*

Idlers, really needs no verification by reference, being just an opinion dropped, and whoever dropped it and when, equally valuable to us—Sainte-Beuve, according to Stevenson, as he grew older, came to regard all experience as a single great book, in which to study for a few years before we go hence: and it seemed all one to him whether you should read in Chapter XX, which is the Differential Calculus, or in Chapter XXXIX, which is hearing the band play in the gardens. Note well, if you please, that I am not endorsing this as a word of advice for Tripos purposes.   I am but applying it to Thackeray, who never sat for his degree, but left Cambridge to write *Vanity Fair*, *Pendennis*, *Esmond*, sundry other great stories, with several score of memorable trifles—ballads, burlesques, essays, lectures, *Roundabout Papers*, what-not.   If I may again quote from Sir Walter Raleigh, "there are two Days of Judgment, of which a University examination in an Honours School is considerably the less important."   The learning we truly take away from a University is (as I conceive) the talent, whatever it be, we use (God helping), and turn to account.   Says Mr. Charles Whibley of Thackeray's two years here:

The friendships that he made ended only with his life, and he must have been noble, indeed, who was the friend of Alfred Tennyson and of Edward FitzGerald. Moreover, Cambridge taught him the literary use of the university, as the Charterhouse had taught him the literary use of a public school. In a few chapters of *Pendennis* he sketched the life of an undergraduate, which has eluded all his rivals save only Cuthbert Bede. He sketched it, moreover, in the true spirit of boyish extravagance, which he felt at Cambridge and preserved even in the larger world of London; and if Trinity and the rustling gown of Mr. Whewell had taught him nothing more than this, he would not have contemplated them in vain.

As a matter of fact, of course, the Charterhouse and Cambridge had taught him much more, even of scholarship. "Scholarship," is, to be sure, a relative term which, if lifted to the excellent heights—to scorn lower degrees of comparison—(as heaven forbid it should not be) will exclude all who have so learnt their Horace at school that in after life merely to rehearse and patch together from memory an Ode of his, long ago learnt for "repetition," brings comfort to the soul and can steel it, Romanly, under the stars even on Himalayan outposts. But if there be aught worthy the name of scholarship to have that one author bred into your bones—why, then, I challenge that Thackeray did carry away a modicum of scholarship (and a very pure modicum, too) from school and university. I shall come to his prose cadences by and by, and will say no more of them here than that—in *Esmond* especially, but in general and throughout his prose—they are inconceivable by me save as the cadences of a writer early trained upon Greek and Latin. For blunter evidence, you will find the *Roundabout Papers* redolent—in quotation, reminiscences, atmosphere—of Horace on every page; and for evidence yet more patent take his avowed imitation of Horace (*Odes* i. 38), the two famous, jolly Sapphic stanzas beginning *Persicos odi*. Turn to your Conington (say) and you will find them most neatly and adequately rendered: and then take your Thackeray—

> But a plain leg of mutton, my Lucy,
>   I prithee get ready at three;
> Have it smoking and tender and juicy,
>   And what better meat can there be?

And when it has feasted the master,
'Twill amply suffice for the maid:
Meanwhile I will smoke my canaster,
And tipple my ale in the shade.

Years ago, I discoursed, standing here, on the Horatian Model in English Verse, attempting to show you how this man and that man—Andrew Marvell, for example, and Matthew Prior, had attempted it here and there and how nearly achieved it: of Milton, again, how he tried to build his Sonnet, redeeming it from the Petrarcan love-business upon the model of the Horatian Ode; how some sonnets of his (familiar or political—that *To Mr. Lawrence* for instance, as a specimen in one mode, or those *To the Lady Margaret Ley*, or *On the Late Massacre in Piedmont* as specimens in another) are deliberately, experimentally Horatian; and how narrowly—how very narrowly—William Cowper, by deflection of religious mania, missed to be our purest Horace of all. But Thackeray is of the band. To alter a word of Carlyle's, "a beautiful vein of *Horace* lay struggling about him."

IV

But, to return upon the first of the two "key-secrets" —Disappointment and Religion—and to leave Religion aside for a moment—I cannot find that, save in his domestic affliction, Thackeray can rightly be called a disappointed man. There is of course a sense—there is of course a degree—in which every one of us, if he be worth anything, arrives at being a disappointed man. We all have our knocks to bear, and some the most dreadful irremediable wounds to bind up and hide.

But whatever Thackeray spent or owed at Cambridge
(to pay in due time), he took away, with his experience,
a most gallant heart. He went to London, lost the rest
of his money in journalistic adventures, and fared out
as a random writer, without (as they say) a penny to
put between himself and heaven. What does he write
later on in reminiscence to his mother, but that these
days of struggle were the jolliest of all his life?—

> Ye joys that Time hath swept with him away,
>   Come to mine eyes, ye dreams of love and fun;
> For you I pawned my watch full many a day,
>   In the brave days when I was twenty-one.

That is good gospel. "Fall in love early, throw your
cap over the mill; take an axe, spit on your hands; and,
for some one, make the chips fly."

V

But (say the critics) he was disappointed, soured
because—conscious of his powers of "superior" education and certain gifts only to be acquired through education, he felt that Dickens—whom certain foolish
people chose to talk of endlessly as his rival—was all
the time outstripping him in public favour. Now, as
for this, I cannot see how Thackeray, in any wildest
dream, could have hoped to catch up with Dickens and
pass him in popularity. To begin with, he came to
fruition much later than Dickens: in comparison with
the precocity of *Pickwick* Thackeray was in fact thirty-
seven before he hit the target's gold with *Vanity Fair*.
His earlier serious efforts—*Catherine, Barry Lyndon,
The Book of Snobs*—are sour and green stuff, call them

what else you will. They deal with acrid characters and (what is more) deal with them acridly. But even supposing them to be masterpieces (which title to two of the three I should certainly deny) where was the audience in comparison with that to which Dickens appealed? Where, outside a few miles' radius of Clubland, did men and women exist in any numbers to whom Thackeray's earlier work could, by any possibility, appeal? The dear and maiden lady in *Cranford*, Miss Jenkyns, as you remember, made allowances for *Pickwick* in comparison with Dr. Johnson's *Rasselas*. "Still perhaps the author is young. Let him persevere, and who knows what he may become, if he will take the Great Doctor for his model." But what—what on earth would she have made of *Barry Lyndon*? And what would good Captain Brown himself have made of it? I can almost better see the pair, on the sly, consenting to admire *Tristram Shandy*.

Now Dickens and Thackeray were both thin-skinned men in their sensitiveness to public approbation. On at least one occasion each made a fool of himself by magnifying a petty personal annoyance into an affair of the world's concern. As if *anybody* mattered to that extent!—

> Hi motus animorum atque haec certamina tanta
> Pulveris exigui jactu compressa quiescunt.

But in literary London there are always (I regret to say) busybodies who will estrange great men if they can; and, the cause of quarrel once set up, I still more regret to say that the great men quite as often as not come most foolishly out of it. Thackeray's estrangement from Dickens happened over an article by a young

journalist of twenty-seven—Mr. Edmund Yates, afterwards Editor of *The World*, a society newspaper—and
Thackeray's foolish insistence, in the teeth of remon-
strances by Dickens and Wilkie Collins, that young
Yates should be expelled from the Garrick Club. A
week before Thackeray's death, he and Dickens met
on the steps of the Athenæum, passed, turned, and
looked at each other. Thackeray held out a hand,
which Dickens did not refuse.

Now may I put in here, Gentlemen, and in parenthe-
sis, a word of which I have often wanted to unburden
myself? . . . Some of you—some of the best of you,
I hope—may leave Cambridge for Fleet Street, a street
which I too have trodden. It is a street of ambitions;
but withal the centre of our English Republic of Letters,
in the motto of which, though there can be no "Equal-
ity," let us neither exclude the "Liberty" that Milton
fought for, nor the "Fraternity" of elder and younger
brethren. I remember this plea for Fraternity being
put up by an eminent man of letters, still with us; and
being so much impressed by it that it outlasted even
the week-after-next, when I found him taking off the
gloves to punish a rival scribe. But these two were
musical critics, arguing about music: and I have sometimes, pondering, thought that there must really be
something naturally akin between music and prosody
(arts of which I know so little), seeing that the professors of both pelt each other in terms of insult so
amazingly similar and with a ferocity the likeness of
which one has to recognise even while murmuring,
"Come, come! What is this all about, after all?" I
suppose the average Musical Review in the weekly
papers to contain more mud to the square inch than
even *The Dunciad!* And you must acknowledge,

Gentlemen, *The Dunciad*, for all its wit, to be on the whole a pretty wearisome heap of bad breeding. It kicks: but as they say in the country, there is "plenty hair on the hoof." What I plead is that all we engaged in *literature* take some warning from the discourtesies of the past, and that you, at any rate, who pass out into literary practice from this Tripos of ours, shall pass out as a confraternity of gentlemen. Consider, if you will, that Literature, our mistress, is a goddess greater than any of us. She is Shakespeare and Ben Jonson too; Milton and Dryden; Swift, Addison, Steele; Berkeley and Goldsmith; Pope and John Gay; Johnson, Gibbon, Burke, Sheridan; Cowper and Burns; Blake and Wordsworth and Coleridge; Landor, Scott, Keats, Shelley and Byron; Carlyle, Ruskin, Tennyson, Browning, all, says the Preacher, "giving counsel by their understanding and declaring prophecies." I name but a few of the procession, but all were her knights; and each, in his time, fought for his ideal of her—

> Blue is Our Lady's colour,
>   White is Our Lord's:
> Tomorrow I will make a knot
>   Of blue and white cords;
> That you may see it where I ride
>   Among the flashing swords.

Or let me lower the key and put it thus—addressing you as plain apprentices and setting the ground no higher than an appeal for the credit of our craft. I once wrote of Robert Louis Stevenson, and with truth, that he never seemed to care who did a good piece of work so long as a good piece of work got itself done. Consider, on top of this, the amount of loss to the world's benefit through those literary broils and squabbles. You are expected, for example, to know something, at least, of *The Dunciad* in your reading for the English Tripos: and I dare say many of you have admired its matchless conclusion:

> Lo! thy dread empire CHAOS is restor'd:
> Light dies before thy uncreating word:
> Thy hand, great Anarch, lets the curtain fall.

But turn your admiration about and consider what a hand capable of writing *so* might have achieved in the long time it had wasted, turning over an immense buck-basket of foul linen. No, Gentlemen—take the example of poor Hazlitt—contemporary misunderstandings, heart-burnings, bickerings make poor material for great authors. I cannot find that, although once, twice or thrice, led astray into these pitfalls, Thackeray (and this is the touchstone) ever really envied another man's success.

"Get *David Copperfield*," he writes in a familiar letter: "by jingo, it's beautiful; it beats the yellow chap (*Pendennis*) of this month hollow."

And again, "Have you read Dickens? Oh, it's charming. Bravo Dickens! it (*David Copperfield* again) has some of his very prettiest touches—those inimitable Dickens' touches which make such a great man of him."

In truth there was in this tall fellow of six-feet-four a strain of melancholy not seldom observable in giants.[1]

---

[1] He was remarkable for height and bulk: a lumbering, unathletic figure with a slouch. One day being at a fair with his friend "Big Higgins" (*Jacob Omnium*) they approached a booth and Higgins felt in his pockets for small change. "Oh!" said Thackeray, "they'll pass us in free, as two of the profession."

Add to this that touch of inherited Anglo-Indian melancholy of which I spoke a fortnight ago; add the tragedy
of his marriage; and I think we need not seek amid any
literary disappointments for the well of the song of
"Vanity, vanity, all is vanity" which, springing evident
in the title of his first great novel, runs an undercurrent
through all that he wrote.

It was not for nothing that he translated Uhland's

The King on the Tower

The cold grey hills they bind me around,
　　The darksome valleys lie sleeping below,
But the winds as they pass o'er all this ground,
　　Bring me never a sound of woe!

Oh! for all I have suffered and striven,
　　Care has embittered my cup and my feast;
But here is the night and the dark blue heaven,
　　And my soul shall be at rest.

O golden legends writ in the skies!
　　I turn towards you with longing soul,
And list to the awful harmonies
　　Of the Spheres as on they roll.

My hair is grey and my sight nigh gone;
　　My sword it rusteth upon the wall;
Right have I spoken, and right have I done:
　　When shall I rest me once for all?

O blessed rest! O royal night!
　　Wherefore seemeth the time so long
Till I see yon stars in their fullest light,
　　And list to their loudest song?

VI

This leads us naturally to the second "key-secret"
which Mr. Merivale found in Thackeray—his Religion.
That is all very well, but what do we understand by it?
That Thackeray was very simply devout no reader of
his novels will question for a moment. Philip, for instance, flings himself quite naturally on his knees in
prayer: and, I am sure, quite as naturally did Thackeray
in any moment of trouble, as he might be seen religious-
ly walking with his daughters to public worship. But
again, what is prayer? or what was it to Thackeray?—
forgive me that I raise this question, since religion has
been claimed as one of his two "key-secrets." What is
prayer, then? Is it that which, in Jeremy Taylor,
"can obtain everything," can "put a holy constraint
upon God, and detain an angel till he leave a blessing
. . . arrest the sun in the midst of his course and send
the swift-wing'd winds upon our errand; and all those
strange things, and secret decrees, and unrevealed
translations which are above the clouds and far beyond
the region of the stars, shall combine in ministry and
advantages for the praying man"? Is it with Thackeray so forcible a power as that? Or is it just the
humble yet direct petition of the Athenians, commended by Marcus Aurelius—"Rain, rain, dear Zeus,
on the ploughed fields of the Athenians"—in truth, says
the Emperor, for his part, "we ought not to pray at all,
or to pray in this simple and noble fashion."

There is a considerable difference, you see: and for
my part I have, searching Thackeray's works, no doubt
that Thackeray's prayer was ever direct, devout, un-
abashed and as simple, as anything in *Tom Brown's
School Days* transferred to a big grown man. You may

at most put him down as a guest at the inn of Emmaus.
But he lived through the time of Newman, Manning,
Martineau; and all I can say is that if Religion involve
any conflict at all of the soul, in his novels I detect
nothing of the sort: nothing even resembling those
spiritual tortures which, afflicting men so various and
differing (if you will) in degree as Newman, Clough, and
yet later Richard Jefferies, were a real and dreadful
burden of the soul to our fathers and grandfathers.
Thackeray lived up to the very thick of the conflict: it
touched him not. He was devout just as—shall we
say?—we elders have known certain Anglo-Indian
Captains who went through the Mutiny and during it
saw things upon which, coming home, they locked
their lips, gallant gentlemen!

So Thackeray walked and knelt, as it seems to me
in the very simplest of Creeds. Its summary is no
more—and no less—than old Colonel Newcome's dying
Adsum! Says a reviewer in the *North British:*

We cannot resist here recalling one Sunday evening in
December, when he was walking with two friends along the
Dean road to the west of Edinburgh—one of the noblest
outlets to any city. It was a lovely evening, such a sunset
as one never forgets; a rich dark bar of cloud hovered
over the sun, going down behind the highland hills, lying
bathed in amethystine bloom; between this cloud and the
hills there was a narrow slip of the pure ether, of a tender
cowslip colour, lucid, and as if it were the very body of
heaven in its clearness; every object standing out as if
etched upon the sky. The north-west of Corstorphine
Hill, with its trees and rocks, lay in the heart of this pure
radiance, and there a wooden crane, used in the quarry
below, was so placed as to assume the figure of a cross:
there it was, unmistakable, lifted up against the crystalline

sky. All three gazed at it silently. As they gazed, he gave
utterance in a tremulous, gentle, and rapid voice, to what
all were feeling, in the word "Calvary"! The friends
walked on in silence, and then turned to other things.
All that evening he was very gentle and serious, speaking,
as he seldom did, of divine things,—of death, of sin, of
eternity, of salvation; expressing his simple faith in God,
and in his Saviour.

VII

I shall attempt in another lecture, Gentlemen, to
examine some of Thackeray's limitations as a novelist;
and passing on, to explore the curious, most haunting
felicity of his prose. You will have already gathered
that I am trying to do what all Professors must and no
critic should; which is to discuss an author with whom
he has a broken sympathy. The lilt, the cadence, of
Thackeray's prose are to me a rapture, almost. The
meanness of his concern with life and his cruelty in
handling mean things—as in *A Shabby Genteel Story*—
evoke something like physical nausea. His *Paris
Sketch Book* seems to me about the last word in bumptiousness: his lectures on Swift and on Sterne might,
bating reverence for him even in misdeed, be flipped
as flies are flipped off a clean page of paper. They
needed (as Venables most justly advised) a piano for
accompaniment—or a pianola. On the other hand—
to omit the great novels—his *Roundabout Papers* almost
touch Horatian perfection.

As for his snobbery—well, I promised you that
coming to it, I should waste little of your time. Perhaps I should have called it his "alleged" snobbery,
guardedly (as a cautious non-committal journalist once
wrote of "an alleged School-Treat"), since my own

ears have heard it denied of him. But they have heard with incredulity, since I suppose of this distressing little disease two things to be certain: the first that it is unmistakable, the second that it is incurable. The patient may know—perhaps may feel as acutely as his listeners—that he has it—but in his next sentence it must out: he cannot help himself. Still, it is a human frailty—not ranking in any just condemnation with cruelty (say) or treachery; not worthy to be exalted as a Deadly sin, belonging rather to the peccadilloes about which—if one may misapply Dante's phrase—we do not reason, but give a look and pass on. Moreover, if you followed the argument of my previous lecture, Thackeray's was a venial form of the malady because not deliberately acquired, not (as an American said of side-whiskers) "the man's own fault," but in his blood, inherited of his Anglo-Indian stock. He never—transferred to Chiswick, the Charterhouse, Cambridge, the Temple, Kensington, Pall Mall—eradicated that family sense of belonging to a governing few set amid an alien race, with a high sense of the duty attached to privilege, but without succour of knowing all sorts and conditions of men and understanding them as neighbours; or let me put it, without just that sense which quite stupid men at home acquire in a Rural Council, or the hunting-field, or a cricket-match on the village green.

I wish we could end with that, and just put it (with W. E. Henley) that Thackeray was ever too conscious of a footman behind his chair. Superficially and in estimating him as a man, that were enough for us. But artistically the trouble goes deeper. There is no reason why an artist should or should not take the squalidest of scenes, provided that the story he sets in it is of

serious import. | May we agree that of all atmospheres
the atmosphere of a cheap boarding-house is perhaps
the least inviting—the smell of linoleum and cookery
in the well-staircase, the shabby gentility refurbishing
itself in the small bedrooms, the pretence, the ceremony
at dinner, the *rissoles*, the talk about the Prince of
Wales, the president landlady with "Saturday" written
on her brow? Well, Balzac took this sort of thing and
made masterpieces of it; and Balzac made masterpieces
of it just because he understood that it, also, belonged
to human comedy and tragedy, and that there, as well
as anywhere else, you may find essentially the wreckage
of a King Lear, the dreams of a Napoleon. Thackeray
takes a boarding-house merely to savage it, to empty
one poor chest-of-drawers after another and hang their
pitiable contents on a public wash-line, to hold the
dirty saucepans under our noses, to expose the poor
servingmaid's heart along with her hands, its foolish
inarticulate yearnings along with her finger-nails—
and all for *what?* That is the point—for *what?* To
tell us that her dreams of a fairy prince oscillated
between a flash lodger with a reversible tie and a seedy
artist who dropped his "h's"? We might have guessed
that much, surely, without elaborate literary assistance.
But suppose the thing worth while, why is the man so
cruel about it? His favourite Horace, to be sure, was
cruel to his discarded loves. But here is no revulsion
of lost love. Here is nothing but gratuitous mocking
at a poor girl

> a fifth-rate dabbler in the British gravy—

and nothing else, or nothing we could not have smelt
inside the front door. And he finds *this* worth con-
tinuing and expanding into a long novel of *Philip!*

As a rule, Gentlemen, I hold it idle for a lecturer to talk about an author with whom he has to confess an imperfect sympathy. There are so many others, worth admiring, whom he may help you to admire! But as many of us come to Milton against the grain, conquered by his divine music, so the spell of Thackeray's prose takes me, often in the moment of angriest revolt and binds me back his slave. I shall try, next time, to speak of its great magic.

THACKERAY (III)

I

I FEAR, Gentlemen, that you will have to take my earlier remarks to-day with some sympathy for your lecturer's time of life, even though you refuse that respect for greying hairs which I shall never claim of you. If you hereafter remember at all, you will remember that never from this desk was preached anything but confidence in you, never a word to bind you with any old or middle-aged rules of wisdom. "Earth loves her young," says Meredith:

> Her gabbling grey she eyes askant, nor treads
> The ways they walk, by what they speak oppressed

—which is well and hopeful and in the way of nature. But since Professors do not come by nature you have to forgive them a certain maturity, a date, a crust in the bottle, and handle them gently if you would know the vintage.

I shall ask you, then, to discount what follows in apparent depreciation of Thackeray: to remind yourselves that we are all too prone to destroy the age just preceding our own; with something of that primitive instinct which (they say), translated into legislation amid the South Seas, commands a grandfather to scale a tree and hold on, if he can, while his prehensile young

sway the trunk and jerk it.   I do not myself believe in
these rude communal tests, that they ever were, or
indeed that, even in our time, natural science has
arrived, for instance, at any fixable limit for a Professor's incapacity—and tenacity.

I am simply stating a plain historical fact when I say
that the men who were young and practised writing in
the later days of Queen Victoria—and as devotedly as
any of you can be pract sing it to-day—found their
most peculiar, most dearly cherished, anathema in the
"preachiness" of the *mid*-Victorian novelists—of which
"preachiness" Thackeray had been perhaps the most
eminent practitioner and exemplar.   He confesses it,
indeed, in one of the *Roundabout Papers*.   Says he:

Perhaps of all the novel-spinners now extant, the present
speaker is the most addicted to preaching.   Does he not
stop perpetually in his story and begin to preach to you?
When he ought to be engaged with business, is he not for
ever taking the Muse by the sleeve, and plaguing her with
one of his cynical sermons?   I cry peccavi loudly and heartily.   I tell you I would like to be able to write a story which
should show no egotism whatever, in which there should
be no reflections, no cynicism, no vulgarity (and so forth)
but an incident in every other page, a villain, a battle, a
mystery, in every chapter.

II

That last sentence quite misses the point—or at least
seemed to miss it quite hopelessly to those who were
young in the 'nineties: whose favourite models were
French or Russian—Balzac, Stendhal, Mérimée, Flaubert, de Maupassant, Turgueniev, the Tolstoy of
Sevastopol and *War and Peace*.

It is a long while ago: but passions of faith we had; the first commanding us (poor fellows!) to agonise in search of the right or most expressive word; the second to keep *our*selves out of any given story making the persons exhibit their characters of themselves and by the actions, the actions again explain themselves by what the persons had said or done previously. In other words these young men attempted to apply to the novel Aristotle's dictum concerning the Epic, of which they conceived the novel to be (as Fielding had maintained) the artistic successor. (And here let me advise all you who have read the *Poetics* to study Fielding's reasoned application of that treatise in his prefaces to the several Books of *Tom Jones*):

"Admirable on all counts," says Aristotle, "Homer has the special merit of being the only poet who understands the part he should take himself. In his own person he should intrude as little as possible. It is not in *that* way he imitates life. Other writers force themselves into the business throughout and imitate but little and rarely. Homer, after a few words of preface, at once brings in a man or a woman as it may be, never characterless but each distinctively characteristic."

To put it in another way—and to employ for once a couple of terms which as a rule these discourses banish, a story should be as purely objective as possible, the author's meaning infused indeed (as it must be in any story worth the telling) but his own person, with his own commentary, as rigidly excluded as from a stage-play—say, as from *King Lear* or *Tartuffe*. *Madame Bovary* and *Boule de Suif* were the exemplars (to name but two); any chat by the author himself ranked as an offence against art.

III

Now, just accepting this as a historical fact, without question for the moment of its rightness or wrongness, you will easily see how impatient it made that generation with many things to which their fathers had been prone. Let me mention two or three.

(1) To begin with, it made them abhor those detailed descriptions of hero, heroine and others—those page-long introductions to which the great Sir Walter was prone: the philosophical reason for this being that no art should attempt that which can be far better done by another. "Her hair, of a raven gloss, concealed its luxuriance within the confines of a simple ribbon. Loosened, it fell below her waist. The upper part of her face, with its purely-arched eyebrows, suggested a Cleopatra. A lover of the antique might have cavilled, perchance, at the slight uptilt of the nose, which indeed, etc.: or again at the pout of the pretty, provocative mouth reminiscent"—well, of some picture of Greuze rather than of some statue or other with which the reader was presumably acquainted. "But as she burst upon Harold's vision in a gown of some simple soft white clinging material—" and so on. It seemed that a drawing could do that sort of thing better and, for the reader, in one-twentieth part of the time.

(2) Secondly, our theory cut out long descriptions of "natural scenery." Hardy's preliminary Chapter of Egdon Heath would, of course, be judged for what it was—a deliberate and magnificent setting of slow, perdurable nature as background to the transitory life of man, the stern breast that has suckled so many fretful children and seen them pass. And again, as in *The Woodlanders* all the sap of English woodland—all its

spirits of Dryad and Hamadryad—all its aeolian murmurs in the upper boughs—might be evoked to dignify
a most simple country story. But the sort of romantic-
ism that used to enjoy itself in the Alps, amid thunder-
storms, the solitary communings of the tortured breast
with the grander aspects of peak and ravine, of the
atrabilious or merely bilious, with the avalanche—all
this [shall I call it the Obermann nonsense?] was wiped
out even as the terrors of that gentleman who making
an early ascent of the tall but inconsiderable slope of
Glaramara, sat down and demanded to be "let blood."
In short, lengthy descriptions of scenery passed out of
vogue along with lengthy descriptions of feminine
charms.

(3) Thirdly—and to be very brief about this—the
names of invented characters came to be real, or at
least plausible names. Such names as those with which
Dickens, Thackeray, Trollope, spoilt the verisimilitude
of their novels—"Lord Frederick Verisopht," "Mr.
Quiverful" or the list of Becky's guests in *Vanity Fair*
—"the Duchess Dowager of Stilton, Duc de la Gruyère,
Marchioness of Cheshire, Marchese Allessandro Stra-
chino, Comte de Brie, Baron Schapsugar and Chevalier
Tosti"—all in the slang of that day "quite the *cheese*."
You may say what you like against the old realistic
novel, but anyhow it earned a living in its day if only
by cutting out this detestable boil inherited from
Ben Jonson, with his type names of Brain-worm,
Well-bred, La Foule, Sir Epicure Mammon, and so
on. . . .

(4) But above all this passion of one's youth for
purely objective treatment of narrative fell as a de-
nunciatory curse upon Thackeray's incurable habit of
preaching. And here, if we were right (which I shall

not here contend), we blithely damned ourselves to the permanent unpopularity we are beginning to enjoy. Take warning: for if there be one vice this nation has in its bones it is a fondness for preaching. An inscrutable addiction, an unholy habit! I observe even in railway trains that nine of our nation will swallow a column of propaganda, unashamed in its cookery, for one that will relish a clean news-report. And yet, Gentlemen, the mind that can separate clean news from propaganda and suggestion is the only mind we should seek to send forth from this city of ours, as the only mind that shall save our state.

This awful propensity to preaching!—and but yesterday an attempt to force upon all Professors no less than forty preachments a year—a gluttony of misemployment in a land of unemployed!

Let me illustrate. Robert Louis Stevenson wrote a story, *Treasure Island*, over which a number of those young men of whom I have been talking waxed enthusiastic, just because it told a plain tale neatly as (they held) a tale should be told. But *Treasure Island* cut (as they say) very little ice with the General Public. What fetched the General Public and made Stevenson popular was *Dr. Jekyll and Mr. Hyde*, and that because the General Public read into it a religious lesson which the author had never intended. Thereafter he, having ever in him a strain, as W. E. Henley noted, a

something of the Shorter Catechist,

gave way to preachment—to the composition of collects and Christmas sermons and (as apparently any of us can do—it is a career open to all the talents) thereby attracted audiences. But where had gone the economy of description, the directness of narrative, the sudden incisiveness of a speaking voice? Take this, for example, of the *Hispaniola's* working her way in to anchorage:

All the way in, Long John stood by the steersman and conned the ship. He knew the passage like the palm of his hand; and though the man in the chains got everywhere more water than was down in the chart, John never hesitated once.

"There's a strong scour with the ebb," he said, "and this here passage has been dug out, in a manner of speaking, with a spade."

We brought up just where the anchor was in the chart, about a third of a mile from either shore, the mainland on one side, and Skeleton Island on the other. The bottom was clean sand. The plunge of our anchor sent up clouds of birds wheeling and crying over the woods; but in less than a minute they were down again, and all was once more silent.

The place was entirely land-locked, buried in woods, the trees coming right down to a high-water mark, the shores mostly flat, and the hill-tops standing round at a distance in a sort of amphitheatre, one here, one there. Two little rivers, or rather, two swamps, emptied out into this pond, as you might call it; and the foliage round that part of the shore had a kind of poisonous brightness. From the ship we could see nothing of the house or stockade, for they were quite buried among trees; and if it had not been for the chart on the companion, we might have been the first that had ever anchored there since the island arose out of the seas.

There was not a breath of air moving, nor a sound but that of the surf booming half a mile away along the beaches and against the rocks outside. A peculiar stagnant smell hung over the anchorage—a smell of sodden leaves and rotting tree-trunks. I observed the doctor sniffing and sniffing like some one tasting a bad egg.

"I don't know about treasure," he said, "but I'll stake my wig there's fever here."

You will remark, first, how the mere description moves with the story, following the crew in and just noting the landscape as *they* saw it after the long sea-passage: quite in the fashion of Homer who (as Lessing observed) does not in the *Iliad* weary with any long description of the finished shield of Achilles but coaxes us up to the forge of Hephaestus, so that like the children at the open door of Longfellow's village smithy we see the work shaping under the workman's hammer, and—forgive the trite old verse—

> love to see the flaming forge
> And hear the bellows roar,
> And catch the burning sparks that fly
> Like chaff from a threshing-floor:

quite in the fashion of the *Odyssey*, too, where the Wanderers, *and we with them*, make landfall

> on the foam
> Of perilous seas, in faery lands forlorn

and beach the black ship and disembark and wonder at cliff, glade and waterfall, we wondering (that is) through their eyes.

You will remark, secondly, in the casual passage I quoted, how the very few words spoken—those by John Silver, the villain, those by the Doctor who is the true *punctum indifferens*, the normal sane man of the story as truly as is Horatio in *Hamlet*—bite in, as by sharp acid, the impression of the story—the *meaning* of it, at that moment, to the mutineer and to the simply honest man.

Am I comparing small things with great? Why, Gentlemen, of course I am, and purposely; to convince you, if I can, that in small as in great—the same laws rule true narrative art.

IV

So we come back to Thackeray, and to preaching. Preaching, or lecturing, would seem to be an endemic itch of our nation, first (I am sure) to be cured through attack on the public propensity for listening to lectures and sermons. You will never cure the lecturer. In my own part of the world the propensity to preach is notoriously virulent. As the song puts it, into the mouth of an enthusiastic emigrant—

> And I will be the preacher,
>   And preach, three times a day,
> To every living creature
>   In North Americay.

For a moment let us go back to Thackeray's humbugging protest that he wished he were able to write a story with "an incident in every other page, a villain, a battle, a mystery, in every chapter."

I say (with what reverence it leaves me to command) that this is pure, if unconscious, humbug, and a clouding of truth. For what is an "incident"? A murder—say that of Duncan in the castle of Inverness; a ghost on the battlements of Elsinore, stalking; a horseman in the night, clattering; a ghostly tapping, a detective holding a lantern over a reopened grave—all these are incidents and rather obviously so. But so also, if properly used, may be the tearing-up of a letter, the stiffened drop of a woman's hands, a sigh, a turning-away.

"Since there's no help, come let us kiss and part"— just that, and if you can use that, what more tragic? Thackeray himself—albeit he could borrow hardily enough from Dumas, as when Colonel Esmond breaks his sword—in that very book achieves his topmost height, his most unchallengeable stroke as an artist, by just telling how a brilliant girl steps down a staircase, and ending on two words, half-whispered in French, at the foot of it—as we shall see, by and by.

V

No: I dare to say that this gift of loose, informal, preaching was Thackeray's bane *as a novelist*. The ease with which it came to him, and the public's readiness to accept it, just tempted him to slouch along. *Esmond* and the first half of *Vanity Fair* excepted, he never seems (to me at least) to have planned out a novel. He could not sit at home, in his desolated house, and concentrate himself upon a close-knit artistic design: but wrote, as I have said, in hotels or "upon Club paper," usually behind-time and (as the saying is) with the printer's devil at his elbow: and so this great melancholy man could, out of his melancholy and his genius, curiously matched with it, of vivacious talk summon up ream upon ream at call. Heaven forbid this should suggest that when he came to facts—more especially when he dealt with his beloved eighteenth century— he was careless. On the contrary, he knew it familiarly as a hand knows its glove. I suppose no later writer (with the possible exception of Austin Dobson) has understood the earlier half of that century better. For certain, again, no writer has, comparably with Thackeray, revivified it. Scholars are always on the pad, with dark lanterns, to catch out writers of imagination: but I observe that these Proctors, encountering Thackeray, carefully edge to the other side of the street. I cannot find that anything in *Barry Lyndon*, *Esmond*, *The Virginians*, the opening of *Denis Duval*, has ever been seriously challenged by the pedants: and considering Thackeray's fame and the minute jealousy of pedants, that is a fairly fine record. In the famous chapters on Brussels and Waterloo in *Vanity Fair*, so far as I discover, every record confirms, not one contradicts, his story.

Again, as it seems to me, this feebleness in construction—this letting the story go at hazard and filling out with chat or preaching—this lazy range of invention in plot—matches with limits in the range of his *characters*. Here again he is always impeccable when dealing with an Anglo-Indian retired, whether it be Jos. Sedley or Colonel Newcome—high or low; or with a Foker or a Costigan or anyone he has encountered in his own Bohemian life, or in a Pall Mall Club or in an Irish regiment or in any dingy lodging-house, at home or abroad. Any inhabitant of these haunts, haunts of his actual experience, he can exhibit and experiment upon with infinite variety. Within that range, you can say, he almost never went wrong. He could there convert all particulars to a Universal. No shadow of doubt can rest on the literal and actual truth of an anecdote he puts into *De Finibus*, one of his best *Roundabout Papers*.

"I was smoking," says he, "in a tavern parlour one night, and this Costigan came into the room alive, the very man; the most remarkable resemblance of the printed sketches of the man, of the rude drawings in which I had depicted him. He had the same little coat, the same battered hat, cocked on one eye, the same twinkle in that eye. 'Sir,' said I, knowing him to be an old friend whom I had met in unknown regions—'Sir,' I said, 'may I offer you a glass of brandy-and-water?' '*Bedad ye may*,' says he, '*and I'll sing ye a song tu.*' Of course he spoke with an Irish brogue. Of course he had been in the army. In ten minutes he pulled out an army agent's account, whereon his name was written. A few months later we read of him in a police court. How had I come to know him, to divine him? Nothing shall convince me that I have not seen that man in the world of spirits. . . ."

They used (he adds) to call the good Sir Walter the "Wizard of the North." What if some writer should appear who can write so *enchantingly* that he shall be able to call into actual life the people whom he invents? . . . Well, I think Thackeray could do that: but only, I think, in the small district limited by the Haymarket on the east and Kensington Gardens on the west. He could call spirits from the vasty deep of the Cider Cellars, evoke them from the shadowy recesses of the Reform or the Athenacum Club. But, like Prospero, he had to draw a ring around him before his best incantations worked. The cautious Trollope remarks that his Sir Pitt Crawley "has always been to me a stretch of audacity which I have been unable to understand. But it has been accepted." Yes, to be sure, it has been accepted, and old Sir Pitt is wickedly alive and breathing just because (on Thackeray's own confession) he was drawn from the life. But as a rule, if you take his dukes and duchesses you will find him on ticklish ground, even so far northward as Mayfair, apt (shall we say?) to buttonhole the butler. Always saving *Esmond* and a part of *The Virginians*, I ask you to compare anything in Thackeray with the opening of Tolstoy's *War and Peace*, and you will detect at once which author is dealing with what he supposes and which with what is known to him, so familiar that he cannot mistake his people even as he enters a room.

VI

But now we come to the man's style; by which I mean, of course, his propriety and grace of writing. It is, as we have seen, a "flowing" style: it has that amplitude which Longinus commended and our Burke practised, as an attribute of the sublime. For defect, as a *narrative* style, it tells in three or more pages what might as well be told in three sentences and often better. Without insisting that the writers of the 'nineties (of whom I spoke but now) ever managed to justify their painful search for the briefest, most telling phrase, I submit that it is unlikeliest to be found by a man writing against time, for monthly numbers. That (if you will) being granted, we have to ask ourselves *why* Thackeray's prose is so beautiful that it moves one so frequently to envy, and not seldom to a pure delight, transcending all envy. For certain the secret lies nowhere in his grammar, in which anyone can find flaws by the score. Half the time his sentences run as if (to borrow a simile of Mr. Max Beerbohm's concerning Shakespeare's *A Midsummer-Night's Dream*) the man were kicking up a bedroom slipper and catching it again on his toe. The secret lies, if you will follow his sentences and surrender yourselves to their run and lull and lapse, in a curious haunting music, as of a stream; a music of which scarce any other writer of English prose has quite the natural, effortless, command. You have no need to search in his best pages, or to hunt for his purple patches. It has a knack of making music even while you are judging his matter to be poor stuff; music—and frequent music—in his most casual light-running sentences. I protest, Gentlemen, I am not one of your *pereant qui ante nos nostra dixerunt* fellows: I grudge no man saying a thing of mine before me, even when I know it *must* be valuable because the anticipator is Mr. George Saintsbury; and so far am I from wishing him to perish that one of my sustaining hopes of life is that of congratulating him on his hundredth birthday. (Do not be afraid: in any event, it shall not be from this desk.) But I protest also that in his *History of English Prose Rhythm* he surprised a secret which was mine, and shy as love—the conviction that for mastery—unconscious, native mastery, it may be—of "that other rhythm of prose"—no English writer excels Thackeray, and a very few indeed approach him. So you guess that I have to deal at once with a sense of gratitude and a grudge that my secret can now stand expressed and confirmed by so high an authority: and my grudge I shall work off by quoting him.

"When I say," he affirms, "that I hardly know any master of English prose-rhythm greater, in his way, than Thackeray, and that I certainly do not know any one with so various and pervasive a command, I may seem to provoke the answer, 'Oh! you are, if not a maniac, at any rate a *maniaque*.' Nevertheless, I say it; and will maintain it. The most remarkable thing about Thackeray is his mastery of that mixed style, '*shot* with rhythm.' Even in his earliest and most grotesque extravaganzas you will rarely find a discordant sentence—the very vulgarisms and mis-

spellings come like solecisms from a pair of pretty lips
and are uttered in a musical voice. As there never
was a much hastier writer, it is clear that the man thought
in rhythm—that the words, as they flowed from his pen,
brought the harmony with them. Even his blank verse
and his couplets in prose, never, I think, in any one instance unintentional, but deliberately used for burlesque
purposes, have a diabolical quality and, as the wine merchants say, 'breed' about them, which some very respect-
able 'poets' have never achieved."

He quotes a short beautiful passage from *Vanity
Fair*—

She was wrapped in a white morning dress, her hair
falling on her shoulders and her large eyes fixed and without light. By way of helping on the preparations for
the departure [for Waterloo where let me remind you he,
her husband, was to fall and lie, with a bullet through his
heart], and showing that she too could be useful at a moment so critical, this poor soul had taken up a sash of
George's, from the drawers whereon it lay and followed
him to and fro, with the sash in her hand, looking on
mutely as the packing proceeded. She came out and stood
leaning at the wall, holding this sash against her bosom,
from which the heavy net of crimson dropped like a large
stain of blood.

He proceeds:

Take another and shorter—not, I hope, impudently short
"Becky was always good to him, always amused, never
angry."
Anybody can do that? Perhaps; but please find something like it for me before 1845, and out of Thackeray, if
you will kindly do so. *In* him it is everywhere.

But, for the cadence of it—since all true prose demands prolonged cadences—let me try to read you a passage or two from the exquisite sixth and seventh chapters of *Esmond*. Harry Esmond is home from his campaigning, has been to service in the old cathedral, and meets his dear mistress outside as the service is done and over. Mark, I say, the cadences of that scene of reconciliation—

She gave him her hand, her little fair hand: there was only her marriage ring on it. The quarrel was all over. The year of grief and estrangement was passed. They never had been separated. His mistress had never been out of his mind all that time. No, not once. No, not in the prison; nor in the camp; nor on shore before the enemy; nor at sea under the stars of solemn midnight; nor as he watched the glorious rising of the dawn: not even at the table, where he sat carousing with friends, or at the theatre yonder, where he tried to fancy that other eyes were brighter than hers. Brighter eyes there might be, and faces more beautiful, but none so dear—no voice so sweet as that of his beloved mistress, who had been sister, mother, goddess to him during his youth—goddess now no more, for he knew of her weaknesses; and by thought, by suffering, and that experience it brings, was older now than she; but more fondly cherished as woman perhaps than ever she had been adored as divinity. What is it? Where lies it? the secret which makes one little hand the dearest of all? Who ever can unriddle that mystery? Here she was, her son by his side, his dear boy. Here she was, weeping and happy. She took his hand in both hers; he felt her tears. It was a rapture of reconciliation.

They walked as though they had never been parted, slowly, with the grey twilight closing round them.

"And now we are drawing near to home," she continued, "I knew you would come, Harry, if—if it was but to forgive me for having spoken unjustly to you after that horrid—horrid misfortune. I was half frantic with grief then when I saw you. And I know now—they have told me. That wretch, whose name I can never mention, even has said it: how you tried to avert the quarrel, and would have taken it on yourself, my poor child: but it was God's will that I should be punished, and that my dear lord should fall."

"He gave me his blessing on his death-bed," Esmond said. "Thank God for that legacy!"

"Amen, amen! dear Henry," said the lady, pressing his arm. "I knew it. Mr. Atterbury, of St. Bride's, who was called to him, told me so. And I thanked God, too, and in my prayers ever since remembered it."

"You had spared me many a bitter night, had you told me sooner," Mr. Esmond said.

"I know it, I know it," she answered, in a tone of such sweet humility, as made Esmond repent that he should ever have dared to reproach her. "I know how wicked my heart has been; and I have suffered too, my dear. I confessed to Mr. Atterbury—I must not tell any more. He—I said I would not write to you or go to you—and it was better even that, having parted, we should part. But I knew you would come back—I own that. That is no one's fault. And to-day, Henry, in the anthem, when they sang it, 'When the Lord turned the captivity of Zion, we were like them that dream,' I thought yes, like them that dream—them that dream. And then it went, 'They that sow in tears shall reap in joy; and he that goeth forth and weepeth, shall doubtless come again with rejoicing, bringing his sheaves with him;' I looked up from the book and saw you. I was not surprised when I saw you. I knew you would come, my dear, and saw the gold sunshine round your head."

She smiled an almost wild smile as she looked up at him. The moon was up by this time, glittering keen in the frosty sky. He could see for the first time now clearly, her sweet careworn face.

"Do you know what day it is?" she continued. "It is the 29th of December—it is your birthday! But last year we did not drink it—no, no. My lord was cold, and my Harry was likely to die: and my brain was in a fever; and we had no wine. But now—now you are come again, bringing your sheaves with you, my dear." She burst into a wild flood of weeping as she spoke: she laughed and sobbed on the young man's heart, crying out wildly, "bringing your sheaves with you—your sheaves with you!"

So they fare to the lit house, and to the tragedy which is the tragedy of all womankind; of beauty fading while desire endures, the passion to be loved persists; most tragic of all when a mother meets in a daughter her careless conquering rival.

As they came up to the house at Walcote, the windows from within were lighted up with friendly welcome; the supper-table was spread in the oak parlour; it seemed as if forgiveness and love were awaiting the returning prodigal. Two or three familiar faces of domestics were on the look-out at the porch—the old housekeeper was there, and young Lockwood from Castlewood, in my lord's livery of tawny and blue. His dear mistress pressed his arm as they passed into the hall. Her eyes beamed out on him with affection indescribable. "Welcome," was all she said, as she looked up, putting back her fair curls and black hood. A sweet rosy smile blushed on her face; Harry thought he had never seen her look so charming. Her face was lighted with a joy that was brighter than beauty— she took a hand of her son, who was in the hall waiting his mother—she did not quit Esmond's arm.

"Welcome, Harry!" my young lord echoed after her.

"Here we are all come to say so. Here's old Pincot: hasn't she grown handsome?" and Pincot, who was older, and no handsomer than usual, made a curtsey to the Captain, as she called Esmond, and told my lord to "Have done, now."

"And here's Jack Lockwood. He'll make a famous grenadier, Jack; and so shall I; we'll both 'list under you, Cousin. As soon as I am seventeen, I go to the army— every gentleman goes to the army. Look! who comes here—ho, ho!" he burst into a laugh. "'Tis Mistress Trix, with a new ribbon; I knew she would put one on as soon as she heard a captain was coming to supper."

This laughing colloquy took place in the hall of Walcote House, in the midst of which is a staircase that leads from an open gallery, where are the doors of the sleeping chambers: and from one of these, a wax candle in her hand, and illuminating her, came Mistress Beatrix—the light falling indeed upon the scarlet ribbon which she wore, and upon the most brilliant white neck in the world.

Esmond had left a child and found a woman, grown beyond the common height, and arrived at such a dazzling completeness of beauty, that his eyes might well show surprise and delight at beholding her. In hers there was a brightness so lustrous and melting, that I have seen a whole assembly follow her as if by an attraction irresistible: and that night the great Duke was at the playhouse after Ramillies, every soul turned and looked (she chanced to enter at the opposite side of the theatre at the same moment) at her, and not at him. She was a brown beauty: that is, her eyes, hair and eyebrows and eye-lashes were dark: her hair curling with rich undulations, and waving over her shoulders; but her complexion was as dazzling white as snow in sunshine; except her cheeks, which were a bright red, and her lips, which were of a still deeper crimson. Her mouth and chin, they said, were too large and full, and so they might be for a goddess in marble, but not for a woman whose eyes were fire, whose look was love, whose voice was the sweetest low song, whose shape was perfect symmetry, health, decision, activity, whose foot as it planted itself on the ground was firm but flexible, and whose motion, whether rapid or slow, was always perfect grace—agile as a nymph, lofty as a queen—now melting, now imperious, now sarcastic—there was no single movement of hers but was beautiful. As he thinks of her, he who writes feels young again, and remembers a paragon.

So she came holding her dress with one fair rounded arm, and her taper before her, tripping down the stair to greet Esmond.

"She hath put on her scarlet stockings and white shoes," says my lord, still laughing. "Oh, my fine mistress! is this the way you set your cap at the Captain?" She approached, shining smiles upon Esmond, who could look at nothing but her eyes. She advanced holding forward her head, as if she would have him kiss her as he used to do when she was a child.

"Stop," she said, "I am grown too big! Welcome, Cousin Harry," and she made him an arch curtsey, sweeping down to the ground almost, with the most gracious bend, looking up the while with the brightest eyes and sweetest smile. Love seemed to radiate from her. Harry eyed her with such a rapture as the first lover is described as having by Milton.

"N'est-ce pas?" says my lady, in a low, sweet voice, still hanging on his arm.

Esmond turned round with a start and a blush, as he met his mistress's clear eyes. He had forgotten her, rapt in admiration of the *filia pulcrior*.

I have said some hard things, Gentlemen, upon Thackeray and have indicated some dislike of him here and there, or, at least, some impatience. But to the man who could at once so poignantly and so reticently

bring those two scenes into contrast—with all its meaning—*all* meaning—modulated to so perfect a balance
of heart and intelligence wedded in human speech—
well, to that man I conclude by bowing the head,
acknowledging a real master: a great melancholy man
with his genius running in streaks, often in thin streaks
about him but always, when uttered, uttered in liquid
lovely prose.

THE VICTORIAN BACKGROUND

I

I INTEND, in this and two following lectures Gentlemen, taking my illustrations in the main from Victorian times, to examine with you how one and the same social question, urgent in our politics, presented itself to several writers of imaginative genius, all of whom found something intolerable in England and sought in their several ways to amend it.

At the beginning of this enquiry let me disclaim any *parti pris* about the duty of an imaginative writer towards the politics of his age. Aristophanes has a political sense, Virgil a strong one even when imitating Theocritus; Theocritus none: yet both are delightful: Lucretius has no care for politics, Horace has any amount, and both are delightful again: the evils of his time which oppress the author of *Piers Plowman*, affect Chaucer not at all: Dante is intensely political, Petrarch, far less sublime as a poet, disdains the business; Villon is for life as it flies, Ronsard for verse and art (and the devil take the rest); Spenser, with a sore enough political experience, casts it off almost as absolutely as does Ariosto. Shakespeare has a strong patriotic sense and a manly political sense: but he treats politics—let us take *King John* and *Coriolanus* for examples—artistically, for their dramatic value. He knows about

The oppressor's wrong, the proud man's contumely

and that they can be unendurable: but he does not use them for propaganda (odious word!) whatever the minute of utterance. Milton put all his religion into verse, his politics into prose; save for a passage or two in *Lycidas* and *Paradise Lost* he excluded politics from his high poetry. On the other hand Dryden had a high poetic sense of politics, and it pervades the bulk of his original poetry, while the opening of his famous *Essay of Dramatic Poesy* strikes an introductory note as sure as Virgil's, through whom a deep undercurrent of politics runs from the first page of the *Eclogues* to the last of the *Æneid*. Our poets of the eighteenth century were social and political in the main: since if you once take Man for your theme, you, or some one following you, must be drawn on irresistibly to compare the position you assign him in the scheme of things with his actual position in the body politic, to consider the "Rights of Man," "man's inhumanity to man" and so forth. *An Essay on Man* (with the philosophy Pope borrowed for it) leads on to *The Deserted Village:*

> Ill fares the land, to hast'ning ills a prey,
> Where wealth accumulates and men decay

—to Crabbe's Poor House, Hall of Justice, Prison; to Blake's lyrical laments over small chimney-sweeps, blackamoors, foundlings and all that are young and desolate and oppressed, and the vow to sweep away "these dark Satanic mills" (of which I shall have more to say by and by) "and build Jerusalem in England's green and pleasant land." Turn now to Keats and

you are returned upon *mere* poetry, in the Latin sense
of *mere*. Keats has no politics, no philosophy of state-
craft, little social feeling: he is a young apostle of
poetry for poetry's sake.

> Beauty is truth, truth beauty,—that is all
> Ye know on earth, and all ye need to know.

But of course, to put it solidly, that is a vague observation—to anyone whom life has taught to face facts and
define his terms, actually an *uneducated* conclusion,
albeit most pardonable in one so young and ardent.
Let us, for a better, go on to the last and grandest word
of his last, unfinished, poem:

> "High Prophetess," said I, "purge off
> Benign, if so it please thee, my mind's film."
> "None can usurp this height," returned the Shade,
> "But those to whom the miseries of this world
> *Are* misery, and will not let them rest."

Such a spirit, preëminently, was Shelley; of whom,
when the last word of disparagement has been said, or
the undeniable truth, put into a phrase by Mr. Max
Beerbohm, "a crystal crank," the equally undeniable
fact remains that Shelley suffered tortures over the
woes of his fellow-creatures, while Byron (for a contrast) cares scarcely at all for the general woe surround-
ing him, everything for his own affliction in a world
which had paid him tribute far above the earnings of
common men, and yet not only (as Shelley does) casts
the blame on tyrants and governments, but the *cure* for
his egoistical troubles on political machinery, revolu-
tions. I go on, taking names and illustrations almost

at random. Contrast any Radical utterance of Tennyson's—his *Lady Clara Vere de Vere*, for example—with poor Thomas Hood's *Song of the Shirt*. Why, it fades away: Hood's passionate charity simply withers up the other's personal self-assertive inverted snobbery. If you have stuff in you, contrast the note of

> With fingers weary and worn,
>   With eyelids heavy and red,
> A woman sat, in unwomanly rags,
>   Plying her needle and thread

with the whine of *Lady Clara Vere de Vere*—

> The grand old gardener and his wife
> Laugh at the claims of long descent

—which is just

> When Adam delved, and Eve span,
> Who was then the gentleman?

—on the pianola. Observe, pray, that I am not comparing the poetic *gift*, in which (as in other gifts of the gods) Tennyson very greatly outweighted Hood. I am merely setting some poets against others and contrasting the degrees in which they exhibit social or political sensitiveness. We should all allow, probably, that Robert Browning was a greater poet and a stronger thinker than his wife: but probably deny to him the acute indignation against human misery, social wrong, political injustice, evinced by the authoress of *The Cry of the Children* or *Casa Guidi Windows*. Of the two friends, Matthew Arnold and Arthur Hugh Clough, we should as probably admit Arnold to be the better poet as Clough to be the less occupied with his own soul, the more in vain attempt to save other men. So again among the Pre-Raphaelites Swinburne raves magnificently for the blood of tyrants: but when it came to lifting the oppressed, to throwing himself into the job, what a puff-ball was he beside William Morris who had announced himself as no more than "the idle singer of an empty day"!

One fishes in the night of deep sea pools:
    For him the nets hang long and low,
Cork buoyed and strong: the silver gleaming schools
        Come with the ebb and flow
    Of universal tides, and all the channels glow.

Or holding with his hand the weighted line
    He sounds the languors of the neaps,
Or feels what current of the springing brine
        The cord divergent sweeps,
    The throb of what great heart bestirs the middle deeps.

Thou also weavest meshes, fine and thin,
    And leaguer'st all the forest ways:
But of that sea, and the great heart therein
        Thou knowest nought: whole days
    Thou toil'st, and hast thy end—good store of pies and
        jays.

II

So far we have spoken of poets—fairly selected, I trust—and have found that there are poets and poets; and some are Olympian in attitude, looking down deep below the surface from a great height as a gannet spies his fish; but high aloof, concerned rather with universal themes than with the woman of Canaan clamorous in

the street crying for her daughter, "Truth, Lord: yet
the dogs eat of the crumbs which fall from their masters' table."

Now if we turn to our novelists, from Defoe to Scott,
we find that the novel from its first virtual beginning in
our country and for a century or more, has for social
diseases in the body politic little concern and practi-
cally no sense at all. Defoe has strong political sense,
but keeps it for his tracts and pamphlets: in *Robinson
Crusoe* (and specially in the third volume, *The Serious
Reflections of Robinson Crusoe*), in *Moll Flanders*, in
Roxana, he is always a moralist, but a religious moralist. If—to twist a line of *Hamlet*—there's something
rotten in the *state* of Denmark, it does not come within
the scope of the novelist whose office is to combine
amusement with general edification. So—leaving out
the edification—it is in *Tristram Shandy*, so in *The
Vicar of Wakefield*. Richardson is all for the human
heart as he reads it, and female virtue. Fielding with
his genial manly morality—Fielding, magistrate of a
London Police Court, and a humane one—discloses
little sense in his novels of any *vera causa* in our system
supplying the unfortunates for whom, in daily life,
he tempers justice with mercy. You will not, I think,
cite *Jonathan Wild* against me. Noble fellow, as he
drops down the Thames—stricken to death, and knowing it—on that hopeless voyage to Lisbon, his thoughts
are hopeful for England and the glory of her merchant
shipping: and (says he) it must be our own fault if it
doth not continue glorious:

for continue so it will, as long as the flourishing state of our
trade shall support it, and this support it can never want,
till our legislators, shall cease to give sufficient attention

to the protection of our trade, and our magistrates want sufficient power, ability, and honesty to execute the laws: a circumstance not to be apprehended, as it cannot happen till our senates and our benches shall be filled with the blindest ignorance, or with the blackest corruption.

Smollett's recipe for a novel is just a rattling picaresque story enlivened by jocular horse-play. Respect Fanny Burney and idolise Jane Austen as we will, they move their plots on a narrow and sheltered stage: while the romantics, working up from Horace Walpole to Scott, call in the past to redress the poverty of the present and the emptiness of a general theory of the arts which, deservedly sovereign in its day, has passed by imitation into convention, and through convention, as always, into mere inanition.

III

Now if you will take, as a convenient starting-point for your enquiry, the year 1832—the year that saw the passing of the Great Reform Bill and the death of Scott: if you will start (I say) with that year beyond which, when I first made acquaintance, with the English School here, our curiosity was forbidden to trespass—you will find that then, or about then, certain terrible diseases in our Commonwealth were brewing up to a head. As everyone now recognises, we must seek the operating cause of these in what we now agree to call the "Industrial Revolution"; that is in the process as yet unrestricted by law, encouraged by economic theory, moving at once too fast for the national conscience to overtake or even to realise it and with a step of doom as rigidly inexorable as the machinery, its agent and its symbol, converting England into a manufacturing country, planting the Manchester of those days and many Manchesters over England's green and pleasant land, and leaving them untended to grow as they pleased polluting her streams, blackening her fields, and covering—here lies the indictment—with a pall of smoke, infinite human misery: all this controlled and elaborated by cotton-lords and mine-owners who prospered on that misery.

The plight of rural, agricultural, England is another story.   Here in Lancashire, Derbyshire, Yorkshire was a monstrous revolution gathering strength (as I say) beyond men's power even to realise it.   And if they realised it, there was Political Economy assuring them that it had to be.   And it continued (as you will remember) long after poor Wragg strangled and left her illegitimate infant on the dismal Mapperly hills and the egregious Mr. Roebuck asked, if, the world over or in past history, there was anything like it.   "Nothing.   I pray that our unrivalled happiness may last."

We all recognise it now, and the wicked folly of it —or at least I hope we do.   My purpose to-day, Gentlemen, is not to excite vain emotions over a past which neither you nor I can remedy at all, but simply to show that—as, after all, we are a kindly nation—the spectacle of industrial England about and after 1832 became intolerable to our grandfathers: how it operated upon two extraordinarily different minds: and (if I can) how irresistible is the wind of literature, through what mouthpiece soever it breathes with conviction.

IV

But before examining how two of the most dissimilar minds conceivable—one a man's, the other a woman's

—reacted upon it, I must indicate the enormity of the challenge.

France had passed through her Revolution and her Terror, with graphic details of which our public speakers and writers had taken pains to make our country familiar enough: and England had won out of the struggle, having taken the side she chose, all oblivious (as we are, maybe, to-day) that victory in arms is at best but the beginning of true victory, and that she herself was in the throes of a revolution not a whit the less murderous than that of France, and only less clamant because its victims, instead of aristocrats and politicians and eminent saviours of their country following one another by scores in tumbrils to die scenically in the Place de la République, the Place of the Guillotine, were serfs of the cotton-mill and the mine, wives, small children, starved unscenically, withered up in foetid cellars or done to death beside the machines of such a hell-upon-earth as Manchester had grown to be out of towns in which an artificer, however humble, had once been permitted to rejoice in that which alone, beyond his hearth and family, heartens a man—the well-executed work of hand and brain. The capitalists of that time simply overwhelmed these towns, expanding, converting them into barracks for workers. Who these workers were, let an advertisement in a Macclesfield paper of 1825 attest—

To the Overseers of the Poor and to families desirous of settling in Macclesfield. Wanted between 4,000 and 5,000 persons between the ages of 7 and 21 years.

Yes, let us pass the hideous towns with but one quotation, from Nassau Senior—

As I passed through the dwellings of the mill-hands in Irish Town, Ancoats and Little Ireland, I was only amazed that it was possible to maintain a reasonable state of health in such homes. The towns, for in extent and number of inhabitants they are towns, have been erected with the utmost disregard of everything except the immediate advantage of the speculative builder. . . . In one place we found a whole street following the course of a ditch, because in this way deeper cellars could be secured without the cost of digging, cellars not for storing wares or rubbish, but for dwellings of human beings. Not one house in the street escaped the cholera.

"Such," wrote Chadwick, that careful observer, "is the absence of civic economy in some of our towns that their condition in respect of cleanliness is almost as bad as that of an encamped horde or an undisciplined soldiery."

But from the poor men and women—who had *sold* themselves into these slums and industrial slavery—let us turn to their hapless children, who, after all, had never asked to be born. Your Malthus in that age, and your Mr. Harold Cox in this, are positive (God forgive them!) that a number of these brats never ought to be born. (I don't know the price of millstones, but they ought to be cheap and handy, and properly labelled.) I shall lay stress on these children, Gentlemen, because—as children do so often—they brought back the gospel—or something of it. For these weaklings, *as they were the foundation of the manufacturer's wealth, by their illimitable woe enabling him to cut his wages*, in the end brought about his exposure. To us—for always to us in our day the past wears a haze softening it into sentiment—Elizabeth Barrett Browning's *Cry of the Children* is nothing, or suspected as sentimental, to be classed alongside with anything (say)

by Mrs. Hemans or L. E. L.   Listen to a couple of
stanzas or three—

"For oh," say the children, "we are weary,
  And we cannot run or leap;
If we cared for any meadows, it were merely
  To drop down in them and sleep.
Our knees tremble sorely in the stooping,
  We fall upon our faces, trying to go;
And underneath our heavy eyelids drooping
  The reddest flower would look pale as snow.
For, all day, we drag our burden tiring
  Through the coal-dark, underground;
Or, all day, we drive the wheels of iron
  In the factories, round and round.

For all day the wheels are droning, turning;
  Their wind comes in our faces,
Till our hearts turn, our head with pulses burning,
  And the walls turn in their places:
Turns the sky in the high window, blank and reeling,
  Turns the long light that drops adown the wall,
Turn the black flies that crawl along the ceiling:
  All are turning, all the day, and we with all.
And all day the iron wheels are droning,
  And sometimes we could pray,
'O ye wheels' (breaking out in a mad moaning),
  'Stop! be silent for to-day!'"

And well may the children weep before you!
  They are weary ere they run;
They have never seen the sunshine, nor the glory
  Which is brighter than the sun.
They know the grief of man, without its wisdom;
  They sink in man's despair, without its calm;
As slaves, without the liberty in Christdom,
  As martyrs, by the pang without the palm . . .

Let them weep! let them weep!

They look up with their pale and sunken faces,
    And their look is dread to see,
For they mind you of their angels in high places,
    With eyes turned on Deity.
"How long," they say, "how long, O cruel nation,
    Will you stand, to move the world, on a child's heart,—
Stifle down with a mail'd heel its palpitation,
    And tread onward to your throne amid the mart?
Our blood splashes upward, O gold-heaper,
    And your purple shows your path!"
But the child's sob in the silence curses deeper
    Than the strong man in his wrath.

V

Now, I dare say some of you, even while I read
this, were dismissing it in your minds as early-Victorian humanitarianism, faded philanthropy, outworn
sentiment. Yes, but even a sentiment, if it works
simultaneously upon a generation of great and very
dissimilar writers, is a fact in the story of our literature
—a phenomenon, at least, which made itself an event—
to be studied by you scientifically. One of the first
rules of good criticism, and the sheet-anchor of the
historical method, is to put yourself (as near as may be)
in the other fellow's place: and if you take but a very
little pains to do so, you will soon discover that Mrs.
Browning was not writing "for the fun of the thing,"
exuding, or causing to be exuded, any cheap tears.
We are accustomed to Manchester to-day: we take it
for granted as a great community with a most honourable Press to represent its opinions. But we only take
it for granted because it has become tolerable, and it

only became tolerable, then dignified—it only became a city—because our Victorian writers shamed its manufacturers out of their villainies. In the twenties, thirties, and "hungry forties" of the last century Manchester was merely a portent, and a hideous portent, the growth of which at once fascinated our economists and frightened our rulers. Think of the fisherman in the *Arabian Nights* who, unstopping the bottle brought ashore in his net, beheld a column of smoke escape and soar and spread, and anon and aloft, overlooking it, the awful visage of a Genie. Even so our economists watched an enormous smoke ascend from Manchester and said, "Here is undreamed-of national prosperity"; while our ministers stared up into the evil face of a monster they had no precedent to control. You understand, of course, that I use "Manchester" as a symbolic name, covering a Lancashire population which grew in the first twenty years of the century from 672,000 to 1,052,000. But let a very different person from Mrs. Browning—let Benjamin Disraeli, then a young man, describe the portent.

From early morn to the late twilight our Coningsby for several days devoted himself to the comprehension of Manchester. It was to him a new world, pregnant with new trains of thought and feeling. In this unprecedented partnership between capital and science—

Mark you, not between capital and labour, but between capital and science, still by machinery arming capital to vaster strength—

In this unprecedented partnership between capital and science, working on a spot which Nature had indicated as the fitting theatre for their exploits, he beheld a great source of the wealth of nations which had been reserved for these times, and he perceived that this wealth was rapidly developing classes whose power was imperfectly recognised in the constitutional scheme, and whose duties to the social system seemed altogether omitted

—"*and whose duties to the social system seemed altogether omitted.*" There, in Disraeli's words, you have it. Every prolonged war raises a new governing class of prosperous profiteers who turn their country's necessity to glorious gain. So it was a hundred years ago at the conclusion of the long Napoleonic struggle: so it is to-day. So it goes on ever. A profiteering class of speculators and (as Cobbett would say) "loan-mongers" emerges at the top of any great war. Ex-soldiers tramp the roads for work, for bread. Decent folk, bred in the incurable belief that England, whoever suffers, must pay her debts, sell out and suffer, breaking up old homes, cutting neighbourly ties, disappearing, taxed out of endurance electing to suffer, for honour's sake. Succeeds a generation or two which, at school or University, are baptised into the old honourable cult. The gravity of an Englishman, because they are English after all, revives and takes possession of young hearts, made generous by education, forgetful of old woes. And so in time—give it a couple of generations—the descendants of the sponge and the parvenu will have shed the hair from the hoof, will leap to the summons of *noblesse oblige*, and in their turn make haste to die by Ypres or the Somme, transmitting somehow the mettle of England into a future denied to them.

VI

But you will say that, although this revolt in the better minds of England, a hundred years ago, may be a fact, I have as yet quoted but the evidence of a poetess and a novelist.   Very well, then: I go to Blue Books and the reports of several commissions, reminding you that I lay most stress on the children because it happened through their almost inconceivable sufferings that, such as it was, victory came.

In 1831 Michael Sadler (a great man, in spite of Macaulay, and the ancestor of a great one—if I may insert this word of long admiration for the first senior man who spoke to me at my first undergraduate dinner in Hall, more than forty years ago)—in 1831 this Michael Sadler, member for Newark, introduced a Ten Hours Bill, and moved its second reading in a speech that roundly exposed, along with other woes of the poor, the sacrifice of child life in the mills.   The Bill was allowed a second reading on condition that the whole subject should be referred to a Select Committee, over which Sadler presided.

Now let me quote a page from Mr. and Mrs. Hammond's recently published study of Lord Shaftesbury, then Lord Ashley, who, though so many have laughed at him, devoted his life that they should laugh if they chose, but willy-nilly on the right side of their mouths, and not with a grin unacceptable to any Divinity presumed as having created Man in His image—

The Report of Sadler's Committee is a classical document; it is one of the main sources of our knowledge of the conditions of factory life at the time.   Its pages bring before the reader in the vivid form of dialogue the kind of life that was led by the victims of the new system.   Men and women who were old at twenty, from all the industrial districts, from Manchester, from Glasgow, from Huddersfield, from Dundee, from Bradford, from Leeds, passed before their rulers with their tale of weariness, misery,

and diseased and twisted limbs. A worsted spinner of
Huddersfield, Joseph Hebergram, aged seventeen, described his day's work at the age of seven. His hours were
from five in the morning to eight at night, with one solitary
break of thirty minutes at noon. All other meals had to
be taken in snatches, without any interruption of work.
"Did you not become very drowsy and sleepy towards the
end of the day and feel much fatigued?" "Yes; that
began about three o'clock; and grew worse and worse,
and it came to be very bad towards six and seven." "What
means were taken to keep you at your work so long?"
"There were three overlookers; there was one a head
overlooker, and there was one man kept to grease the machines, and there was one kept on purpose to strap." His
brother, who worked in the same mill, died at sixteen from
spinal affection, due to his work, and he himself began to
grow deformed after six months of it. "How far do you
live from the mill?" "A good mile." "Was it very painful for you to move?" "Yes, in the morning I could
scarcely walk, and my brother and sister used, out of kindness, to take me under each arm, and run with me to the
mill, and my legs dragged on the ground; in consequence
of the pain I could not walk." Another witness, an over-
seer in a flax spinning mill at Dundee, said that there were
nine workers in the room under his charge who had begun
work before they were nine years old, and that six of them
were splay-footed and the other three deformed in other
ways. A tailor at Stanningley, Samuel Coulson, who had
three daughters in the mill, described the life of his household when the mill was busy. In the ordinary time the
hours were from six in the morning to half-past eight at
night; in the brisk time, for six weeks in the year, these
girls, the youngest of them "going eight," worked from
three in the morning to ten or half-past ten at night.
"What was the length of time they could be in bed during
those long hours?" "It was near eleven o'clock before we
could get them into bed after getting a little victuals, and

then at morning my mistress used to stop up all night, for fear that we could not get them ready for the time; sometimes we have gone to bed and one of us generally awoke." "Were the children excessively fatigued by this labour?" "Many times; we have cried often when we have given them the little victualling we had to give them; we had to shake them, and they have fallen asleep with the victuals in their mouths many a time."

Another witness, Gillett Sharpe, described how his boy, who had been very active and a good runner, gradually lost the use of his limbs at the mill. "I had three steps up into my house, and I have seen that boy get hold of the sides of the door to assist his getting up into the house; many a one advised me to take him away; they said he would be ruined and made quite a cripple; but I was a poor man, and could not afford to take him away, having a large family, six children under my care."

—and so on, and so on. Sadler forced the horrible tale upon Parliament. Unhappily, being pitted against Macaulay at Leeds in the General Election of 1832, he lost his seat, though Manchester sent an appeal signed by 40,000 factory-workers: and he never returned to the House of Commons. He died in 1835 at fifty-five, worn out by his work on behalf of these poor children.

VII

His mantle descended to Lord Ashley: and Ashley, after bitter defeats, won on the mine-children what had been lost in the cotton-mills. For the mines took an even more hideous toll of childhood than did the mills. Listen to this, extracted from the Report of the Commission of 1840–1842, which shocked all England by its disclosures—

In every district except North Staffordshire, where the younger children were needed in the Potteries, the employment of children of seven was common, in many pits children were employed at six, in some at five, and in one case a child of three was found to be employed. Even babies were sometimes taken down into the pits to keep the rats from their fathers' food. The youngest children were employed as trappers; that is, they were in charge of the doors in the galleries, on the opening and closing of which the safety of the mine depended. For the ventilation of the mine was contrived on a simple principle; there were two shafts, one the downcast, the other the upcast. A fire was lighted at the foot of the upcast to drive the air up the shaft, and air was sucked down through the downcast to fill the vacuum. This air was conducted by means of a series of doors through all the workings of the mine on its passage to the upcast, and these doors were in the charge of a little boy or girl, who sat in a small hole, with a string in his or her hand, in darkness and solitude for twelve hours or longer at a time. "Although this employment," reported the Commission, "scarcely deserves the name of labour, yet as the children engaged in it are commonly excluded from light, and are always without companions, it would, were it not for the passing and re-passing of the coal carriages, amount to solitary confinement of the worst order."

Children were also employed to push the small carriages filled with coals along the passages, and as the passages were often very low and narrow, it was necessary to use very small children for this purpose. "In many mines which are at present worked, the main gates are only from 24 to 30 inches high, and in some parts of these mines the passages do not exceed 18 inches in height. In this case not only is the employment of very young children absolutely indispensable to the working of the mine, but even the youngest children must necessarily work in a bent position of the body." As a rule the carriages were pushed along small iron railways, but sometimes they were drawn by children and women, "harnessed like dogs in a go-cart," and moving, like dogs, on all fours. Another children's task was that of pumping water in the under-bottom of pits, a task that kept children standing ankle-deep in water for twelve hours. In certain districts children were used for a particularly responsible duty. In Derbyshire and parts of Lancashire and Cheshire it was the custom to employ them as engine men, to let down and draw up the cages in which the population of the pit descended to its depths and returned to the upper air. A "man of discretion" required 30s. a week wages; these substitutes only cost 5s. or 7s. a week. Accidents were, of course, frequent,—on one occasion three lives were lost because a child engineman of nine turned away to look at a mouse at a critical moment,—and the Chief Constable of Oldham said that the coroners declined to bring in verdicts of gross neglect from pity for the children.

VIII

Do you ask "What has all this to do with literature, or what has literature to do with these things"? I answer that, as a matter of mere history, literature in the nineteenth century did immensely concern itself with these things: and I add that, as literature deals with life, so if it deserve a place in any decent state, it *should* deal with these things. And to this again I add, because they dealt righteously and unsparingly with these things, Shelley, Dickens, Carlyle, Ruskin—yes and, later, William Morris—live on the lips of men to-day. For they let in light upon dark places; not only revealing them to the public conscience, but, better still and better far, conveying light and waking eyesight in the victims themselves.

Denunciation has its uses: and if you want to hear denunciation, listen to Carlyle—

British industrial existence seems fast becoming one huge poison-swamp of reeking pestilence physical and moral; a hideous *living* Golgotha of souls and bodies buried alive; such a Curtius' gulf, communicating with the Nether Deeps, as the Sun never saw till now. These scenes, which the *Morning Chronicle* is bringing home to all minds of men,—thanks to it for a service such as Newspapers have seldom done,—ought to excite unspeakable reflections in every mind. Thirty-thousand outcast Needlewomen working themselves swiftly to death; three million Paupers rotting in forced idleness, *helping* said Needlewomen to die: these are but items in the sad ledger of despair.

Thirty-thousand wretched women, sunk in that putrefying well of abominations; they have oozed-in upon London, from the universal Stygian quagmire of British industrial life; are accumulated in the *well* of the concern, to that extent. British charity is smitten to the heart, at the laying-bare of such a scene; passionately undertakes, by enormous subscription of money, or by other enormous effort, to redress that individual horror; as I and all men hope it may. But, alas, what next? This general well and cesspool once baled clean out to-day, will begin before night to fill itself anew.

Yes, denunciation has its uses: and public exposure is salutary, or at least sanitary, though its first revelations sicken to such despair as Carlyle's. But the true operation of light is upon the sufferer's own eyes, the promise in its salutation is for them. Listen to this one sentence from Porter's *Progress of the Nation*, published in 1851—

In 1839, 1840 and 1841, 40 per cent. of the men and 65 per cent. of the women married or witnessing marriages in Lancashire and Cheshire could not sign their names

NO EDUCATION

—and at this time Leonard Horner Inspector of Factories, reported that in an area of thirty-two square
miles comprising Oldham and Ashton, with a population of 105,000, there was not a single public day school
for poor children.   Consider these millions of children
who grew up to be men and wives in purlieus not once
penetrated by so much as a glint of the romance, the
poetry, that as we look back—you a short way, Gentlemen—I a long one—we see as Heaven lying about us
in *our* infancy.   *There* lay the soul's tragedy—

The singers have sung, and the builders have builded,
    The painters have fashioned their tales of delight;
For what and for whom hath the world's book been gilded,
    When all is for these but the blackness of night?

There lay the tragedy: there the seat of cure: and if,
with so much left undone, it has become possible from
this desk to preach, without serious rebuke, that
humanism can be taught even in our Elementary
Schools, and, further, that to see it is so taught may well
concern even a great University, these humanitarians
of the nineteenth century were the men and women
who invaded the borders of Zabulon and Nephthalim,
until for them which sat in darkness, in the region and
shadow of death, light is sprung up.

IX

But I recall myself to my purpose; which in two
following lectures shall be as literary, as merely critical,
as I can keep it.   To-day I have set out the theme and
tried to show you how it had perforce to occupy men's
minds and—since artists and imaginative writers must

have feelings as well as intellect—almost to dominate our literature and art in the last century. In that domination of interest you will find implicit, and will easily evolve for yourselves, the reason why the novel in particular, being a social form of art and lending itself in so many ways to episode, discussion, even direct preaching, became political as it never was in the days of Richardson and Fielding, Scott and Jane Austen. The preponderance of the theme being granted, I next propose to examine how it took possession of two persons of genius: a man and a woman; the man assertive, personally ambitious, full of fire and opulent phrase: the woman staid, self-abnegating, to me wearing the quiet, with the intensity, of a noble statue. I can conceive, if one would trace in literature the operation of a compelling idea, no two exponents more essentially disparate than Benjamin Disraeli and Elizabeth Gaskell.

DISRAELI

I

FOR two reasons or (shall we say) against two main obstacles, both serious, Benjamin Disraeli found it hard to gain the ear of Parliament and, having gained it, had yet a long fight before attaining office. To begin with, his race and reputation were against him. He was a Jew, and he had written novels. He was admittedly clever to excess: but cleverness, specially when tainted by literary skill, is, of all others, the reputation which our British Senate most profoundly (and perhaps on the whole wisely) distrusts. That the House "hates a man who makes it think" was the observation of a cynic, no doubt. But I have also heard it said by one long a member of it, that a speaker there must always count on somebody—he knows not whom—who knows the subject more thoroughly than he. Its instinct being for solidity, it shrinks from brilliance as a danger: and this was specially true of the party to which Disraeli allied himself—upon which, we may say, he thrust himself—a Jew, an adventurer, an ambitious, esurient fellow without any stake in the country. What had a party, which didn't in the least object to being called stupid, to gain by the support of such an outsider?

And it is obvious that, for Parliamentary success,

Disraeli had to overcome something more serious—a certain bumptiousness of manner, a youthful confidence and ease in Sion, helped out by elaborate ringlets, mannerisms and a foppish dress very much overdone: an opulence of speech and waistcoat, both jarring on the very men—and probably most upon these—into whose less-oiled heads he was fighting to drive some ideas. There is a great deal of tactlessness in the story of Disraeli, right up to the moment of Peel's fall. But the story witnesses not only to a growing mastery, won by amazing courage, over the House but—better—to a discipline won over himself.

II

Now as Disraeli, being a novelist, was naturally suspect among the party with whom he had chosen to cast his political lot, so his books were naturally suspected and unjustly treated by his opponents throughout his lifetime: and for this again we may decide that he was largely to blame. He was, as you know, the son of a man of letters: as he puts it, "born in a library, and trained from early childhood by learned men who did not share the passions and prejudices of our political and social life." In his early work, such as *The Young Duke* or *The Infernal Marriage*, we find, with all its excess—the excess of youth—a hard literary finish. Let me quote from the last-named story a few sentences for specimen:

The next morning the Elysian world called to pay their respects to Proserpine. Her Majesty, indeed, held a drawing-room, which was fully and brilliantly attended. . . . From this moment the career of Proserpine was a series of magnificent entertainments. The principal Elysians vied with each other in the splendour and variety of the amusements which they offered to the notice of their Queen. Operas, plays, balls and banquets followed in dazzling succession. Proserpine who was almost inexperienced in society, was quite fascinated. She regretted the years she had wasted in her Sicilian solitude: and marvelled that she could ever have looked forward with delight to a dull annual visit to Olympus; she almost regretted that, for the sake of an establishment, she could have been induced to cast her lot in the regal gloom of Tartarus. Elysium exactly suited her.

Now that, in its way, is as neat as can be. You perceive at once that the style is literary and controlled. Nor, even in the tumultuous close of *Vivian Grey*, his first work, can you fail to perceive that, though exuberant, it was at first controlled. He says:

I have too much presumed upon an attention which I am not able to command. I am, as yet, but standing without the gate of the garden of romance. True it is that, as I gaze through the ivory bars of its golden portal I would fain believe that, following my roving fancy, I might arrive at some green retreats hitherto unexplored, and loiter among some leafy bowers where none have lingered before me. But these expectations may be as vain as those dreams of youth over which we have all mourned. The disappointment of manhood succeeds to the delusions of youth: let us hope that the heritage of old age is not despair.

Analyse that, and you will find it youthful, orientally luxuriant, but well bridled, on the whole, to the cadence of good prose. Press your analysis a little further, and

you will detect the voice of a born rhetorician even in
its first sentence.   Let me add but two words to it:

I have too much presumed, Mr. Speaker, upon an attention which I am not able to command.

—and you have the House of Commons before you,
with Peel and Macaulay, Palmerston and Lord John
Russell, listening.   Even so early his vocation can be
detected as calling, enticing Disraeli away from the
stern discipline of letters to the easier success of rhetoric,
from the sessions of silent thought to the immediate
response of an auditory, whether in Parliament or at
the foot of the hustings.   As even the noblest, most
impassioned sentences of Cicero, addressed to Senate
or law-court, wear a somewhat artificial, attitudinising
air to us in comparison (say) with a colloquy of Socrates
meditated and colloquially reported by Plato, so,
speaking as one who has recently had to search for true
prose, as we conceive it, among the speeches of British
orators, I promise but a thin harvest to the researcher:
the simple reason being that oratory plays to the
moment, literature to thoughts and emotions carried
away, reconsidered, tested, approved on second thought
and in solitude.   Not forgetting many purple patches
in Chatham, his son, Fox, Sheridan, Canning, Bright,
Lincoln, Gladstone and Disraeli himself, I yet assure
you that nowhere—save with the incomparable Burke—
you will find great gleaning on that many-acred field.
And Burke, our glorious exception, was "the dinner-bell
of the House" when he rose to speak.   I fancy that the
most of our legislators when lately seeking re-election
would have avoided a Burke—and wisely.

I shall have more to say of this before I conclude.

For the moment I am but concerned to point out to you that Parliamentary practice laid a double trap for Disraeli as a writer: the first inherent in that practice, the second a peculiar temptation for him.

"It is only by frequent and varied iteration," says Herbert Spencer somewhere, "that unfamiliar truths can be impressed upon reluctant minds": and who has ever served, for example, on a County Council and not felt the iron of that truth penetrate his soul? How true must it have been of a young man, brilliant but suspected, kept out of office on suspicion, preaching a new creed not so much to the benches opposite or into the necks of a distrustful ministry, but hammering it, rather, upon the intelligence of supporters scarcely less distrustful while infinitely more stupid! Can any conceivable task tempt more to that redundancy which destroys a clean literary style?

Now for the man himself.—He was an Oriental and proud of it (let *Tancred*, in particular, attest), of a race but lately admitted to the House of Commons and, if for that reason only, challenged to display himself in debate. With a courage perhaps unexampled in Parliamentary story he let himself go, took the risk, triumphed. But the dyer's hand must inevitably acknowledge, sooner or later, its trade. Now of all practitioners in English writing, a man of Oriental mind and upbringing has to beware of this—that no Occidental literature, since Greece taught it, will suffer ornament as an addition superinduced upon style: and, after some experience, I put it quite plainly —if harshly, yet seriously for his good—to any Indian student who may be listening to these words—that extraneous ornament in English is not only vapid, but ridiculous as the outpouring of a young Persian lover

who, unable equally by stress of passion and defect of
education to unburden his heart, betakes himself to a
professional letter-writer; who in his turn (in Newman's words)—

dips the pen of desire into the ink of devotion and proceeds
to spread it over the page of desolation. Then the night-
ingale of affection is heard to warble to the rose of loveliness
while the breeze of anxiety plays around the brow of
expectation.

"That," says Newman, "is what the Easterns are said
to consider fine writing": and Disraeli, yielding to that
Oriental temptation, will give you, again and again,
whole passages that might have been hired, to depict
the stateliest homes of England, from any professional
penman in any Eastern bazaar.

Speaking, in the Preface to *Lothair*, of his early
work, Disraeli himself admits that much of it (and
Vivian Grey in particular) suffers at least from affecta-
tion. "Books written by boys, which pretend to give
a picture of manners and to deal in knowledge of human
nature, *must*," he says, "be affected. They can be,
at the best, but the results of imagination acting on
knowledge not acquired by experience. Of such cir-
cumstances exaggeration is a necessary consequence,
and false taste accompanies exaggeration." Yes, but
Lothair appeared in 1870, when its author had been
Prime Minister, and had certainly acquired by experience much knowledge of the world and human
nature: and the trouble is that in this very book the
youthful exaggeration not only persists but has exaggerated itself ten-fold, that the Eastern flamboyancy
is more flamboyant than ever. Take, for example, the

following description of the ducal breakfast-table at
Brentham—

The breakfast-room at Brentham was very bright. It
opened on a garden of its own, which at this season was so
glowing, and cultured into patterns so fanciful and finished, that it had the resemblance of a vast mosaic. The
walls of the chamber were covered with bright drawings
and sketches of our modern masters and frames of interesting miniatures, and the meal was served at half-a-dozen
or more round tables which vied with each other in grace
and merriment. . . .

—as well, one may pause to observe, as in rotundity.
These half-a-dozen or more round tables were

brilliant as a cluster of Greek or Italian republics. . . .
After breakfast the ladies retired to their morning room.

We have already been told what they did there—

One knitted a purse, another adorned a slipper, a third
emblazoned a page. Beautiful forms in counsel leant over
frames glowing with embroidery, while two fair sisters
more remote occasionally burst into melody, as they tried
the passages of a new air which had been communicated
to them in the manuscript of some devoted friend.

On the other hand

the gentlemen strolled to the stables, Lord St. Aldegonde
lighting a Manilla cheroot of enormous length. As Lothair
was very fond of horses, this delighted him.

—the cheroot, apparently.

The stables at Brentham were rather too far from the house, but they were magnificent, and the stud worthy of them. It was numerous and choice, and, above all, it was useful. It could supply a readier number of capital riding horses than any stable in England. [Advt.] Brentham was a great riding family. In the summer season the Duke delighted to head a numerous troop, penetrate far into the country, and scamper home to a nine o'clock dinner. All the ladies of the house were fond and fine horsewomen. The mount of one of these riding parties was magical. The dames and damsels vaulted on their barbs and genets and thorough-bred hacks with such airy majesty: they were absolutely overwhelming with their bewildering habits and bewitching hats.

Now, whatever else we say of that, it belongs—does it not?—to the *Arabian Nights* rather than to English acres and the line of English fiction. It is Bluebeard bewitching his guests—his next bride among them— with a delicious *fête-champêtre*. Nay, can you not imagine our poor English Duke gripping the back of his ducal head in the endeavour to recognise himself as leader of this cavalcade? It almost defies parody. Even Thackeray could but make fun of it, in *Codlingsby*, by opposition of scene rather than by caricature of style; by transferring the style merely and maliciously to an old clothes shop in Holywell Street, as thus—

They entered a moderate-sized apartment—indeed Holywell Street is not above a hundred yards long, and this chamber was not more than half that length—and fitted up with the simple taste of its owner.

The carpet was of white velvet—(laid over several webs of Aubassun, Ispahan, and Axminster, so that your foot gave no more sound as it trod upon the yielding plain than the shadow did which followed you)—of white velvet painted

with flowers, arabesques and classic figures by Sir William
Ross, J. M. W. Turner, Mrs. Mee and Paul Delaroche, etc.

"Welcome to our snuggery, my Codlingsby. We are
quieter here than in the front of the house, and I wanted
to show you a picture. . . . That Murillo was pawned to
my uncle by Marie Antoinette."

III

Disraeli's style, in short, cried aloud for attack by
critics who hated him on other scores.

"Personal influences," wrote he, "inevitably mingle in
some degree with such productions. There are critics
who, abstractedly, do not approve of successful books,
particularly if they have failed in the same style; social
acquaintances also of lettered taste, and especially contemporaries whose public life has not exactly realised the
vain dreams of their fussy existence, would seize the accustomed opportunity of welcoming with affected discrimina-
tion about nothing, and elaborate controversy about trifles,
the production of a friend: and there is always, both in
politics and literature, the race of the Dennises, the Old-
mixons, and Curls, who flatter themselves that by libelling
some eminent personage of their times, they have a chance
of descending to posterity."

This sounds well enough, indeed. But in point of
fact Disraeli has a persistent habit of wrapping up his
incomparable gift of irony in language so detestably
fustian that even a fair critic has to search his periods
carefully, separating the true from the sham. A fine
ear will separate them: but it needs a fine ear, and will
tax it the most of its time. All his life, in letters as in
politics, he posed somewhat as a Man of Mystery: and
your Man of Mystery must take the rough with the

smooth: and your Cagliostro or even your honest merchant who talks at once too floridly and too cleverly
cannot blame any plain auditor for suspecting that he
talks, all the while, with his tongue in his cheek.

It is a pity: for I do not see how any fair-minded
reader of Disraeli's novels can fail to acknowledge, at
this distance of time, that the man was eminently
serious, and in earnest, and wise even.   I spoke to you,
a fortnight ago—at too great a length, you may think—
of the problem of industrial England and how the misery
of the poor, caught in its machinery, forced itself
through the imaginative sympathy of certain writers
upon the national conscience: and especially (you may
remember) I spoke of the children because the children
won the battle.   As Francis Thompson says, "The
grim old superstition was right.   When man would
build to a lasting finish, he must found his building over
a child."

Well, I see no reason to doubt—no reason either in
his writings or his public action—that Disraeli's concern over this industrial misery was ever less than disinterested, sincere, even chivalrous.   No one can deny
the sincerity, at least, of *Sybil;* no one the terrible
authenticity of its descriptive pages—such as the
famous picture of a gang emerging from a coal-mine:
for research has shown that throughout and almost
sentence by sentence the author has been at silent
pains to document the almost incredible evidence of
his own eyes with evidence from Blue Books and
Parliamentary Reports.   I shall not harrow your
feelings by reading the passage, having harrowed them
(as I say) sufficiently a fortnight ago.   But you may
take it for the moment—as you may amply satisfy
yourselves by enquiry later and at leisure—that the

Inferno is faithfully depicted: that the mill-owners Shuffle and Screw (Disraeli had a foible for such names and for running them in double harness—you will recall those celebrated duettists, Taper and Tadpole)—that the exactions of these men were real exactions, that the sufferings of the handweaver Warner and his starving family are sufferings that did actually break actual human hearts and that even the upbringing of the factory urchin Devilsdust is not only true to fact but typical. You may be excused for doubting as you read how Devilsdust—so he came to be called, for he had no legitimate name—"having survived a baby-farm by toughness of constitution, and the weekly threepence ceasing on his mother's death," was thrown out into the streets to starve or be run over: how even this expedient failed—

The youngest and feeblest of the band of victims, Juggernaut spared him to Moloch. All his companions were disposed of. Three months' play in the streets got rid of this tender company. . . .

You shudder as you read how the cholera visited the cellar where he and other outcasts slept, until

—one night when he returned home he found the old woman herself dead and surrounded only by corpses. The child before this had slept on the same bed of straw with a corpse: but then there were also breathing things for his companions. A night passed only with corpses seemed to him itself a kind of death. He stole out of the cellar, quitted the quarter of pestilence, and, after much wandering, lay down at the door of a factory.

—where he was taken in, not from charity, but because a brat of five was useful. Do you tell yourself that

Disraeli exaggerates? Then turn to Hansard and read that before Hanway's Act the annual death-rate among these pauper children was estimated at something between 60 and 70 per cent.: that this Act, as Howlett grimly put it, caused "a deficiency of 2,100 burials a year": that the London parishes by custom claimed a right to dispose at will of all children of a person receiving relief, and disposed of them to the manufacturers; and that one Lancashire mill-owner agreed with a London parish to take one idiot with every twenty sound children supplied.[1]

IV

Man, as Aristotle tells us, is a political animal: and among imaginative writers in the 'thirties and 'forties of the last century, Disraeli had an eminently political mind. I say, "eminently," because in the years that followed the great struggle over the Reform Bill all men's eyes—eyes of advocates as of opponents—were turned on this wonderful Reformed Parliament, awaiting some transformation of our society, for good or for evil. The expectancy operated on Disraeli as on the rest. He was a House of Commons man with his ambition centred on success in that House. He did not believe that this reformed House was in any way capable of producing a millennium. With his own purpose very steadily set to advance his career; with a sense of intrigue and a courage steadily sharpened by disappointment; he perceived the nostrums of the new Parliament to be nostrums no more honest than the old; as he perceived the counteracting devices of his

[1] *The Town Labourer, 1760–1832*, by Mr. and Mrs. Hammond, p. 145. From Horner's Speech, *Hansard*, June 6, 1815.

own party to be no more than delaying devices devoid
of principle. He hated the very name of "the Conservative Party" invented by Croker:

I observe, indeed, a party in the State whose rule is to
consent to no change until it is clamorously called for,
and then instantly to yield; but these are *Concessionary*,
not Conservative principles. This party treats institutions
as we do our pheasants, they preserve but to destroy.

But he felt, with the feeling of England, that this evil
of the factory system demanded an instant redress only
to be achieved by sharp legislation: and, so far he was
right. Ashley and his backers could look nowhere but
to Parliament for immediate cure. There happen from
time to time in the history of a nation (as sensible men
must admit) crises to which hasty methods must be
applied, as you catch up and spoil a valuable rug to
smother an outbreak of fire.

V

We know how Disraeli, in those days, saw the full
problem. Here was a country, this England, divided
into Two Nations, the rich and the poor. Here were
the nobles who should, by all *devoir*, be the saviours of
the State, standing by while the middle-class manufacturer held the poor in misery; standing by while the
authority of the Crown diminished under steady depression by the Whigs; standing by while Churchmen
fought for preferment, neglecting the oppressed, for
whom—by every teaching of Christ—a true disciple is
a trustee. You all know, I doubt not, the main persons
and principles of the Young England party which
rallied to Disraeli's call. The men were all younger

than he; mostly of Eton and Cambridge—foremost George Smythe, later Viscount Strangford, most brilliant of all, Lord John Manners, Alexander Baillie Cochrane "the fiery and generous Buckhurst" of *Coningsby*. All of them figure, under other names, in *Coningsby*, and, while that novel is remembered, will be identified in its pages; that is, long after human memory has ceased to care for the personal romance of young men once so chivalrous and admired—

> The expectancy and rose of the fair state,
> The glass of fashion and the mould of form.

But the tenets of this Young England party which gathered so eagerly about the maturer man, Disraeli, were these, as you know: the King stood over all, with his prerogative to be vindicated. His rightful vindicators were our ancient nobility, and their task was to exalt, to sustain him as protector of the poor, and so to restore the peasantry of England (including its mill-hands, famished families, pauper children) to the supposedly happy conditions once enjoyed in the golden age of the monasteries, but forfeit under the oppression of middleclass "industrialists," as we should now term them. I find, for my part, no real evidence of this golden age of the monasteries, and suspect the glow they reputedly shed over a consented medieval country-side to be very vastly enlarged by the mist of romance. But whatever they might or might not have been, their lethargy could never have matched, for evil, the active cruelty of the new system. The monasteries were dead, anyhow: the mills and the mines were grinding lives into death by tens of thousands under men's eyes. Disraeli *knew* how the bringing up of a Devilsdust turns the grown man into a Chartist, and a danger. Disraeli understood Chartists.

VI

In September, 1841, Peel (who owed it to him) refused Disraeli office. We need not go into that tortuous story, or the rights of it this way or that. The point for us is that his exclusion gave him leisure to write *Coningsby*.

What were his qualifications, what his disqualifications in writing *Coningsby?*

To begin with the disqualifications—(1) He had the haziest notion of constructing a plot. From first to last he never gets beyond an idea, and a string of episodes. (2) His hero is, for all his recommendation, an invariable nincompoop, and his heroine (Sybil particularly) not of flesh and blood: not even an embodiment of an idea; a dream of it rather. Coningsby does very much less than justice to Smythe, a man of failings and infinite wit; while in *Lothair* you will pass whole pages in which the hero's contribution to the wisdom of the world amounts to "You don't say so," "I am more than a little surprised," "I have never looked into this matter upon which Your Grace sheds for me, I confess, an entirely new light." You may say that the heroes and heroines of most Victorian novels are puppets conducted through adversity to a chime of marriage bells. But Disraeli deliberately presenting his heroes and heroines as grandiose creatures of ineffable charm, has never the art to make them justify this by what they do or say. Their golden, or raven, hair hangs down their back, and there it ends. Lastly his prose lapses, as the rhetorician's hand becomes subdued to what it works in, into sentences more and more slipshod: while fatuities abound, such as the exclamation, at the beginning of a chapter, "What wonderful things are events!"

So far the devil's advocate. . . . But set against this, first and in front of it, the great fact that an inventor is great not only because he does a thing well, but because he could do it at all. Disraeli in *Coningsby* invented the political novel: and I know nothing to compare with that book unless it be his own *Endymion* in which so touchingly an old man, dejected from political office and power, seeks back with all his worldly wisdom, as one walking out into a garden in a lunar light of memory, to recapture the rose of youth. Of the trilogy—*Coningsby, Sybil, Tancred*—I confess, tracing it backward, that I have small use for *Tancred*, having (be it confessed) not only a stark insensibility to Disraeli's enthusiasm for a mongrel religion neither of his breed nor of mine, but a constitutional aversion to the Lion of Judah considered as a pet. *Sybil*, in addition to its most vivid pictures of the factory poor, has at least a score of pages which no student of the art of writing in English can afford to neglect—take for example its *tour de force* in exhibiting the rise of the Marney family and the successive ennoblements of John Warren, club waiter, and his progeny, through Sir John Warren, and Lord Fitz-Warene, to Earl de Mowbray of Mowbray Castle. The juxtaposition of the selfish and opulent Marney household with the wretched mines, close by, from which they drew their wealth, is admirably managed. But, as I have said, the heroine is but a shadowy figure, and I find the hero little more lively: the pair of them "made for a purpose," and that purpose propaganda. No: *Coningsby* is the masterpiece: and Peel's refusal which led to its composition—Peel's own fatal loss, as it turned out— is our delightful gain. You will easily find, in almost any period of our prose literature since Defoe, a more noble novel: and if one goes back to early romance and thinks (say) of a page of Malory—well, it rebukes the sensual rapture. But, for all that, I defy you to find a more vivacious, a more scintillating book—scintillating with joyful and irresistible malice. At the turn of any page you may happen on such a gem as this:

Lord and Lady Gaverstock were also there, who never said an unkind thing of anybody: her ladyship was pure as snow: but, her mother having been divorced, she ever fancied she was paying a kind of homage to her parent by visiting those who might some day be in the same predicament.

It dares history, and will, for a whole chapter, recount the fall of a Government, the passing of a Bill, the formation of a Cabinet, unravelling actual intrigue, carrying you along by sheer logic as though you galloped with Dumas' Three Musketeers. Disraeli could not invent a character: but he could at once disguise and reveal one borrowed from life. In *Coningsby* he had actual men made to his hands, to prompt the apotheosis or the caricature. He sentimentalises his young friends, and the sense beneath the sensibility may be read in the last paragraph of *Sybil*. What he could do with an enemy let the portrait of Rigby attest.

VII

In *Coningsby* he invented the Political Novel. That this *partus masculus* came so late to birth in our literature, as that it has begotten few successors, admits (as Sir Thomas Browne would say) no wide solution. Genius is rare, anyhow: the combination of political with literary genius necessarily rarer. Given the two combined, as they were in Burke, you still require, for superadding, the inventive faculty, the mode, and the leisure. Not one man of letters in ten thousand can match Disraeli's close inner acquaintance with his subject. Statesmen, in short, have not the leisure to write. Alcibiades leaves no record of what Alcibiades did or suffered. By a glorious fluke, Peel gave this chance and Disraeli took it.

VIII

For a last word to-day—

Quite apart from genuine coruscation of genius, and almost as widely separating and casting from account that tinsel and tawdriness which all can detect, one feels a mistrust (gnawing, as it were, within our laurel) that even the best page of Disraeli does not belong to *us*. We cannot match it somehow with a racy page of Dryden, or of good Sir Walter Scott, of Izaak Walton, John Bunyan, grave Clarendon, Bolingbroke. Gibbon is artificial enough, heaven knows; yet somehow—and one remembers that he had served in the Hampshire Militia—the scent of the hawthorn is never more afar than a field away, even when he discourses of Tertullian or of Diocletian. From Disraeli's prose—or rather from my sense of it—I can never dispel the smatch of burnt sandalwood, the smell of camels and the bazaar. He officiates, somehow—he, a Prime Minister, over an altar not ours—we admire the oracle, but its tongue is foreign.

Still his fame grows. I observe that, as the incense clears, each successive study of him tells something better. He stands in politics admittedly a champion; in literature, too, a figure certainly not among the greatest, yet as certainly one of the great.

MRS. GASKELL

I

WE think of her habitually—do we not?—by her married title of "Mrs. Gaskell." Who Mr. Gaskell was this generation does not, in an ordinary way, pause to enquire: a neglect which does injustice to a gentleman of fine presence, noble manners and high culture. She was a beautiful woman: they married in 1832, and had children, and lived most happily.

So it is as "Mrs. Gaskell" that we think of her: and I dare to wager that most of you think of her as Mrs. Gaskell, authoress of *Cranford*. Now heaven forbid that anything I say this morning should daunt your affection for *Cranford*, as heaven knows how long and sincerely I have adored it. I have adored it at least long enough and well enough to understand its devotees—for *Cranford* has not only become popular in the sense, more or less, that *Omar Khayyam* has become popular—by which I mean that, at this season or thereabouts, numbers of people buy a copy in limp *suède*, with Hugh Thomson's illustrations, and only hesitate over sending it to the So-and-So's with best wishes on a chilling doubt that they sent it last year, with the identical good wishes—if indeed they are not returning the identical volume they received! Well, let us be merry and careless!—in the course of a week or two these soft bricks will be dropping on every hearth.

But seriously, one finds devotees of *Cranford* everywhere; and especially, in my experience, among scholarly old men. They have *Cranford* written on their hearts, sometimes hardly covering a cherished solution of *The Mystery of Edwin Drood*. *Cranford* and the novels of Jane Austen—you never know how many delightful persons cherish them, have them by heart, pore over their text as over an Ode of Pindar's. And they are fierce, these devotees, as the noble new edition of Jane Austen by Mr. Chapman of the Oxford Press has recently been teaching us. Here are five volumes edited with all the care that study and affection can lavish on the task. Yet from here, there and everywhere lovers start up from firesides—scattered widowers of this dear maiden—challenging over *variae lectiones*, feeling for the hilt on the old hip to champion (we'll say) "*screen*" as the right word against "scene" as printed—

"Swerve to the left, Son Roger," he said,
"When you catch his eyes through the helmet-slit."

It is as serious, almost, as all that: and so it is with *Cranford*, and Miss Jenkyns and Captain Brown and adorable Miss Matty.

Yet, let us admit there are certain works which conquer some of us, we cannot tell why. To go a very long way from *Cranford*, take *Tristram Shandy*. No one can really criticise *Tristram Shandy*, and all pretence to do so is mere humbug. Either you like *Tristram Shandy* (as I do, for one) or you don't, and there's an end to it. My sole complaint against the devotees of *Cranford* is that, admiring it, revelling in it, they imagine themselves to have the secret of Mrs. Gaskell, stop there, and do not go on to explore her other works of which one at any rate I shall presently dare to proclaim to you as the most perfect small idyll ever written in English prose.

II

The sin is the worse because every one acknowledges the *Life of Charlotte Brontë* to be—after Boswell's *Life of Johnson*, admittedly beyond competition—among the two or three best biographies in our language. Conceive the Brontës—not Charlotte alone, but the whole family—the whole of that terrible family in that terrible parsonage at Haworth—as this staid lady, wife of a Unitarian minister, faithfully depicts them— the wastrel son, Branwell: through long nights tearing his own heart out, with his stern old father's, in the bedroom they had, for safety, to occupy together: in the end pulling himself up to *die standing:* the shuddering sisters listening on the stairs; Emily, doomed and fierce, she too in her turn standing up to die.   Consider —I will not say *Wuthering Heights*, or Charlotte's well-known magnificent description, in *Villette*, of Rachel and her tortured acting—but consider if only by illustration of contrast this most maddened poem by Emily—and there are others as tragic—

The Prisoner

Still let my tyrants know, I am not doom'd to **wear**
Year after year in gloom and desolate despair;
A messenger of Hope comes every night to **me**,
And offers for short life, eternal liberty.

He comes with Western winds, with evening's wandering
    airs,
With that clear dusk of heaven that brings the thickest
    stars:
Winds take a pensive tone, and stars a tender fire,
And visions rise, and change, that kill me with desire.

Desire for nothing known in my maturer years,
When Joy grew made with awe, at counting future tears:
When, if my spirit's sky was full of flashes warm,
I knew not whence they came, from sun or thunder-storm.

But first, a hush of peace—a soundless calm descends;
The struggle of distress and fierce impatience ends.
Mute music soothes my breast—unutter'd harmony
That I could never dream, till Earth was lost to me.

Then dawns the Invisible; the Unseen its truth reveals;
My outward sense is gone, my inward essence feels;
Its wings are almost free—its home, its harbour found;
Measuring the gulf, it stoops, and dares the final bound.

O dreadful is the check—intense the agony—
When the ear begins to hear, and the eye begins to see;
When the pulse begins to throb—the brain to think again—
The soul to feel the flesh, and the flesh to feel the chain.

Yet I would lose no sting, would wish no torture less;
The more that anguish racks, the earlier it will bless;
And robed in fires of hell, or bright with heavenly shine,
If it but herald Death, the vision is divine.

Consider, I say, that the authoress of *Cranford* not
only lived with these fierce women and comforted them
as their benign friend, with a comfort that no soul can
give to another without understanding, but portrayed
them (their struggles ended) in a book that combines
the English (even the Victorian English) with the

Greek, a fidelity to awful fact with a serene judgment, a tender mercy—the two so discovering and covering all, that—whether it be in charity or in justice—its core of truth has never been challenged: that it stands yet among the noblest few of English biographies. I put it to you that, if you but set together those two books —*Cranford* and the *Life of Charlotte Brontë*—at once you must recognise the operating hand—the quietly operating hand—of genius. But this, even when Mrs. Gaskell's longer novels are thrown into the scale, has avoided, I think—because she herself is so equable, so temperate—its right recognition. Yes, her very portrait has a Hellenic look, so beautiful it is, so penetrating its calm gaze.

III

Yet maybe you think it strange that I find so much of high Hellenic quality in this quiet lady—born a Stevenson, to be sure—but christened Elizabeth Cleghorn, names not to us reminiscential of Hybla or the Ilissus. Her father was a Unitarian minister, who preached in that capacity, in Dob Lane Chapel, Manchester—which again does not suggest the Acropolis. In 1832 she married a Unitarian minister, son of a prosperous manufacturer, minister to a Chapel in Cross Street, Manchester, and prominent on the Home Missionary Board. For these and some particulars that follow I go to the best sources known to me.[1]

Her married life was one of unbroken happiness.

[1] Sir Adolphus Ward's various Introductions to the Knutsford Edition (8 volumes, published by John Murray) and the article on her in the *Dictionary of National Biography*, by the same writer, whose scholarship, when devoted to this dead lady, reaches to a religious note of chivalry.

Her husband had literary leanings, and in 1838 she writes to Mrs. Howitt, "We once thought of *trying* to write sketches among the poor, *rather* in the manner of Crabbe (now don't think this presumptuous), but in a more beauty-seeing spirit: and one—the only one— was published in *Blackwood*, January, 1837.[1] But I suppose we spoke our plan near a dog-rose, for it never went any further."

So you see that she had already made Manchester her home, and was already interested in the poor.

Also one may interpose here that (without evidence of her portrait) she was acknowledged by all who met her to be a person of quite remarkable beauty, and as little conscious of it as any beautiful woman has any right to be: since as Jaques noted:

> if ladies be but young and fair,
> They have the gift to know it.

Above all, she had the ineffable charm of being the least assertive, the most concerned with others, in any company. I think that of her rather than of any other writing-woman one may quote Mrs. Browning's lines on her Kate—

> I doubt if she said to you much that could act
> As a thought or suggestion: she did not attract
> In the sense of the brilliant or wise: I infer
> 'Twas her thinking for others made you think of her.
>
> She never found fault with you, never implied
> Your wrong by her right: and yet men at her side
> Grew nobler, girls purer, as through the whole town
> The children were gladder that pulled at her gown. . . .

[1] The curious may read it in *Blackwood's Magazine*, Vol. XLI, No. CCIV, or in Sir Adolphus Ward's *Biographical Introduction*.

The weak and the gentle, the ribald and rude,
She took as she found them, and did them all good:
It always was so with her—see what you have!
She has made the grass greener even here . . . with her
    grave.

Such a woman, as I trace her portrait, was Mrs. Gaskell,
and I think the end of the story will confirm my reading
of her.   She made no show: without interfering she saw
beauty in the lives of the poor: she lived with the misery
of Manchester and pitied it; and across a personal
bereavement—or (shall we say?) out of the very anguish of her own breast—she relieved her heart in her
first long book in pity for that place.

In 1844 Mr. and Mrs. Gaskell revisited Festiniog, in
North Wales, a halt of their wedding tour.   They
took their children with them; and at the inn there the
eldest daughter caught the scarlet fever.   Mrs. Gaskell
removed her with her infant brother to Portmadoc,
where he sickened of the fever and died.   It was in
search of an anodyne for sorrow that the mother began
to write *Mary Barton*.   Read that book with just these
two or three facts in your mind, and you will find an
illustration—though it almost shames me to give you
one so poignant—of the way in which the sincerest art
is begotten and brought forth: that is, by lifting one's
own experience up to a Universal, and then bringing it
back to *reclothe* it in imaginary, particular, men and
women.

IV

In two previous lectures, Gentlemen, I have given
you—it may well be *ad nauseam*—the conditions of life

among the industrial poor of that period as they can be gathered from Blue Books and out of Hansard. In my last lecture I tried to indicate how they affected the ambitious (and to that extent selfish) but yet chivalrous mind of Disraeli. I shall be shorter with Mrs. Gaskell, who invents no political novel, but just tells the tale and passes on. But she tells it, and I select here to read to you a passage to illustrate rather how gently and charitably she tells it than to make out the worst of the case, which yet may be found in her pages.

At all times it is a bewildering thing to the poor weaver to see his employer removing from house to house, each one grander than the last, till he ends in building one more magnificent than all, or withdraws his money from the concern, or sells his mill, to buy an estate in the country, while all the time the weaver, who thinks he and his fellows are the real makers of this wealth, is struggling on for bread for his children, through the vicissitudes of lowered wages, short hours, fewer hands employed, etc. And when he knows trade is bad, and could understand (at least partially) that there are not buyers enough in the market to purchase the goods already made, and consequently that there is no demand for more; when he would bear and endure much without complaining, could he also see that his employers were bearing their share; he is, I say, bewildered and (to use his own word) "aggravated" to see that all goes on just as usual with the mill-owners. Large houses are still occupied, while spinners' and weavers' cottages stand empty, because the families that once filled them are obliged to live in rooms or cellars. Carriages still roll along the streets, concerts are still crowded by subscribers, the shops for expensive luxuries still find daily customers while the workman loiters away his unemployed time in watching these things, and thinking of the pale, uncomplaining wife at home, and the wailing children asking in vain for enough of food,—of the sinking health, of the dying life, of those near and dear to him. The contrast is too great. Why should he alone suffer from bad times?

I know that this is not really the case; and I know what is the truth in such matters: but what I wish to impress is what the workman feels and thinks.

But there are earnest men among these people, men who have endured wrongs without complaining, but without ever forgetting or forgiving those whom (they believe) have caused all this woe.

Among these was John Barton. His parents had suffered; his mother had died from absolute want of the necessaries of life. He himself was a good, steady workman, and, as such, pretty certain of steady employment. But he spent all he got with the confidence (you may also call it improvidence) of one who was willing, and believed himself able, to supply all his wants by his own exertions. And when his master suddenly failed, and all hands in the mill were turned back, one Tuesday morning, with the news that Mr. Hunter had stopped, Barton had only a few shillings to rely on; but he had good heart of being employed at some other mill, and accordingly, before returning home, he spent some hours in going from factory to factory, asking for work. But at every mill was some sign of depression of trade! Some were working short hours, some were turning off hands, and for weeks Barton was out of work, living on credit. It was during this time that his little son, the apple of his eye, the cynosure of all his strong power of love, fell ill of the scarlet fever. They dragged him through the crisis, but his life hung on a gossamer thread. Everything, the doctor said, depended on good nourishment, on generous living, to keep up the little fellow's strength, in the prostration in which the fever had left him. Mocking words! when the commonest food in the house would not furnish one little meal. Barton tried credit; but it was worn out at the little provision shops, which were now suffering in their turn. He thought it would be no sin to steal, and

would have stolen; but he could not get the opportunity in
the few days the child lingered. Hungry himself, almost
to an animal pitch of ravenousness, but with bodily pain
swallowed up in anxiety for his little sinking lad, he stood
at one of the shop windows, where all edible luxuries are
displayed; haunches of venison, Stilton cheeses, moulds of
jelly—all appetising sights to the common passer by. And
out of this shop came Mrs. Hunter, his late employer's
wife! She crossed to her carriage, followed by the shopman
loaded with purchases for a party. The door was quickly
slammed to, and she drove way; and Barton returned home
with a bitter spirit of wrath in his heart, to see his only boy
a corpse!

You can fancy, now, the hoards of vengeance in his
heart against the employers. For there are never wanting
those who, either in speech or in print, find it their interest
to cherish such feelings in the working classes; who know
how and when to rouse the dangerous power at their command; and who use their knowledge with unrelenting
purpose to either party.

Now you know from actual evidence given you in
my two previous lectures that this account is not over-
strained. You see how the writer makes allowances;
and how, all allowances made, her thrust is as deadly
as any in Disraeli's *Sybil*.

V

But now comes in the difference. Mrs. Gaskell knew
these people as Disraeli did not. She had lived among
them, and to all the angry protests evoked by *Mary
Barton* she returned, of her knowledge, gentle, but
gently firm answers which could not be refuted.[1] The

---

[1] I should mention here, by the way, on Sir Adolphus Ward's authority, the virtual certainty that before writing her own novel she "had
remained quite unacquainted with both *Coningsby* and *Sybil*."

story, at any rate, exercised at once a "commanding effect," and the width of that effect was attested by translations into many foreign languages—French, German, Spanish, Hungarian and Finnish.

She did not go on to exploit that success, that effect. She had said what she had to say; and having found, in the saying of it, her gift as a writer, she passed on to other things. A very beautiful necklace of novels was the result. But this serene indifference to what might with others have meant a very strong "literary" temptation implied no failing devotion to the poor whose woes the book had, once for all, championed. Some eighteen years later, in 1862–3, a time of trouble came over Manchester and South-west Lancashire in general, which

called forth one of the most notable, and certainly one of the best-organized efforts of goodwill and charity which this country has ever seen. In the long struggle between masters and men, the times of the Lancashire Cotton Famine, due to the outbreak and continuance of the American Civil War, brought about a protracted truce, in which the kindly feelings inspired by the self-sacrificing efforts of many leading employers of manufacturing labour cannot but have counted for much.

I am quoting from Sir Adolphus Ward:

Mrs. Gaskell, whose name had so good a sound among the Lancashire working classes that we hear of an Oldham man regularly bringing his children to gaze upon the house in Plymouth Grove where dwelt the authoress of *Mary Barton*, gave many proofs in these times of trouble of her readiness to help suffering in every way in her power.

The relief problem, in short, claimed her almost entirely during that long tribulation of her people. "We were really glad," she writes to a friend, "to check one another in talking of the one absorbing topic, which was literally haunting us in our sleep, as well as being our first thoughts in wakening and the last at night." In organising, superintending, working sewing-rooms, providing dinners, she would work for six or seven hours of her day.

The shadow of these and other industrial troubles recurs, indeed, in some of the later novels, particularly in *North and South:* but always you see that with her there is no political axe to grind, nor scarce a consciousness of there being any such thing: and this disinterested charitableness leads her, as it were, imperceptibly into regions of which Disraeli, with all his genius, never won ken. The first incentive, I have tried to show, operated on both. But whereas he went off into a life of action—great and powerful action, let all admit—to return in his old age to revisit with *Endymion* the glimpses of the moon and his boyish dreams, this unambitious Victorian lady, having found her literary talent, went on to employ it with a serenity unmoved to worship any idols of the market. Glad of course she was to enjoy and use her gift: very modestly glad (as what true woman or man is not?) of the recognition it brought, but following the path to the end to bequeath to the world several noble novels and three shining masterpieces. Of these, of course, the *Life of Charlotte Brontë* is one and *Cranford* the second: and for the moment I leave you to guess at the third. For the moment I wish you to picture this woman. In her writing, as in her daily life, she had no mannerisms. She copied neither Disraeli, nor Dickens, who also championed the poor and was moreover her encourager and editor; nor the Brontës, for all the spell of their genius; nor Trollope, nor George Eliot; though all were great and flattered her with their admiration. Past them all we see her quietly keeping the tenor of her way. Now and again she seems to falter and ask herself—*herself*, mind you—Is this trouble to speak the simple truth as best I can, without heat, really worth its reward as set against the heat and acrimony it provokes? The strictures passed on her *Life of Charlotte Brontë* gave her, for a time, a distaste for it all. But she wrote on, after a little, and on Sunday, November 12, 1865, killed of a sudden by a pang of the heart—carried away, as her epitaph at Knutsford (which is "Cranford") says, "Without a moment's warning"—she left her writings all just as clean and bright as the bunch of her household keys.

> Who sweeps a room, as for Thy laws,
> Makes that, and the action, fine.

VI

I shall pass the catalogue of these writings very quickly in review. The authoress of *Mary Barton* was hailed at that time, when novels were yet few and even poetry but beginning to recover its strength, by great men and by Dickens especially, who engaged her pen for the first number of his serial adventure, *Household Words*. In 1853 appeared her second important novel, *Ruth* (which possibly influenced Dickens' own *Hard Times*, published a year later). Then in June, 1853, came *Cranford*, made into a book from papers contributed to *Household Words* between December, 1851, and

May, 1853. *North and South* ran in *Household Words*
from September, 1854, to January, 1855, and appeared as
a book, with some slight alterations, in that year. In
that year also (on March 31st) Charlotte Brontë died
and Mrs. Gaskell consented, at the old father's urgent
request, to write the Biography. She gave herself up
to the work and finished it in the spring of 1857. The
strictures on it—truth, as Milton says, never comes into
the world but as a bastard—broke her spirit for a
while for all but occasional writing: and then came the
cotton famine, of which I have spoken, to tax all her
energies. But after the stress of this they revived. In
1863 appeared *Sylvia's Lovers*, in 1863–4 *Cousin Phillis*
in the pages of the *Cornhill Magazine*. In this magazine (August, 1864—January, 1866) followed her last
story, *Wives and Daughters,* published soon after in that
year as an unfinished work. So you see the whole tale
of it lies within the central years of the last century,
beginning with *Mary Barton* in 1848 and ending sharply
just eighteen years after.

VII

I do not propose to discuss the toll of her work this
morning. I wish that those of you who aspire to write,
and are here learning to write, would study it—for two
reasons. For the first, while I admit many flaws, it
seems to me elementally of the best literary breeding,
so urbane it is, so disposedly truthful; so much of the
world, quizzing it; so well aware, all the while, of another. For my second, that here you have, refuting, an
exception to all hasty generalisations about the nineteenth century, the Victorian Age, horsehair sofas, the
Evangelicals, the Prince Consort, the Great Exhibition

of 1851 and all that bagful of cheap rubbish. In 1851 this lady was writing *Cranford:* in 1863 she was writing *Cousin Phillis:* and considering that most lovely idyll, I am moved to ask, "Do you, at any rate, know it, this Sicilian yet most English thing of the mid-nineteenth century?" I am moved to say, "Yes, Keats is lovely, and was lovely to me alas! before ever you were born: but quit your gushing and your talk about 'romantic revivals'—which are but figments invented by fellows who walk round and round a Grecian urn, appraising it scholastically. Quit it, and try to *make* a Grecian urn. The horses on the frieze of the Parthenon are good horses: but you have as good to study to-day or to-morrow if you will but take a short journey out to Newmarket and study them. Which is better?—to watch a gallop between two colts on a heath, or to bend a congested nose over *Ferrex and Porrex?*"

To be classical is not to *copy* the classics: to be classical is to learn the intelligence of the classics and apply just *that* to this present world and particularly to this island of ours so familiar and yet so romantic.

VIII

I spoke, a while back, of *three* masterpieces of Mrs. Gaskell, naming two, leaving you to guess the third. Lay by your *Cranford*, and take up and study *Cousin Phillis*.

I suppose its under.ying sadness has kept it out of popular esteem—this tale of scarcely more than a hundred pages—a pale and shadowy sister of *Cranford*. It has none, or little of *Cranford's* pawky fun: it has not *Cranford's* factitious happy ending. But it beats me to guess how any true critic can pass it over and neglect a thing with all that is best in Theocritus moving in rustic English hearts. And it is not *invented*. It has in all its movements the suggestion of things actually seen—of small things that could not have occurred to any mind save that of an eye-witness—of small *recognitions*, each in its turn a little flash of light upon the steady background of rural England. It is England and yet pure Virgil—as purely Virgilian as the vignette, in the Fourth Georgic, of the old man of Corycus tilling his scanty acres:

nec fertilis illa juvencis
Nec pecori opportuna seges nec commoda Baccho—

who yet brought home his own-grown vegetables at night and cast them on the table, in his mind equal to the wealth of kings. I shall read you two passages—the first of young Paul's introduction, by his cousin Phillis, to her father the ex-minister and Virgilian scholar turned farmer and labouring with his hinds—

"There is father!" she exclaimed, pointing out to me a man in his shirt-sleeves, taller by the head than the other two with whom he was working. We only saw him through the leaves of the ash-trees growing in the hedge, and I thought I must be confusing the figures, or mistaken: that man still looked like a very powerful labourer, and had none of the precise demureness of appearance which I had always imagined was the characteristic of a minister. It was the Reverend Ebenezer Holman, however. He gave us a nod as we entered the stubble-field; and I think he would have come to meet us, but that he was in the middle of giving some directions to his men. I could see that Phillis was built more after his type than her mother's. He, like his daughter, was largely made, and of a fair, ruddy

complexion, whereas hers was brilliant and delicate. His
hair had been yellow or sandy, but now was grizzled.
Yet his grey hairs betokened no failure in strength. I
never saw a more powerful man—deep chest, lean flanks,
well-planted head. By this time we were nearly up to
him; and he interrupted himself and stepped forwards,
holding out his hand to me, but addressing Phillis.

"Well, my lass, this is cousin Manning, I suppose. Wait
a minute, young man, and I'll put on my coat, and give you
a decorous and formal welcome. But—Ned Hall, there
ought to be a water-furrow across this land: it's a nasty,
stiff, clayey, dauby bit of ground, and thou and I must
fall to, come next Monday—I beg your pardon, cousin
Manning—and there's old Jem's cottage wants a bit of
thatch; you can do that job to-morrow, while I am busy."
Then, suddenly changing the tone of his deep bass voice
to an odd suggestion of chapels and preachers, he added,
"Now I will give out the psalm: 'Come all harmonious
tongues,' to be sung to 'Mount Ephraim' tune."

He lifted his spade in his hand, and began to beat time
with it; the two labourers seemed to know both words
and music, though I did not; and so did Phillis: her rich
voice followed her father's, as he set the tune; and the men
came in with more uncertainty, but still harmoniously.
Phillis looked at me once or twice, with a little surprise at
my silence; but I did not know the words. There we five
stood, bareheaded, excepting Phillis, in the tawny stubble-
field, from which all the shocks of corn had not yet been
carried—a dark wood on one side, where the wood-pigeons
were cooing; blue distance, seen through the ash-trees,
on the other. Somehow, I think that, if I had known
the words, and could have sung, my throat would have
been choked up by the feeling of the unaccustomed scene.

The hymn was ended, and the men had drawn off, before
I could stir. I saw the minister beginning to put on his
coat, and looking at me with friendly inspection in his
gaze, before I could rouse myself.

And now let me read you this exquisite passage—there
are many almost as lovely—of Phillis in love, walking
with her cousin Paul—alas! not her beloved.

> We talked about the different broods of chickens, and she
> showed me the hens that were good mothers, and told me
> the characters of all the poultry with the utmost good-faith;
> and in all good-faith I listened, for I believe there was a
> great deal of truth in all she said. And then we strolled
> on into the wood beyond the ash-meadow, and both of us
> sought for early primroses and the fresh green crinkled
> leaves. She was not afraid of being alone with me after
> the first day. I never saw her so lovely, or so happy. I
> think she hardly knew why she was so happy all the time.
> I can see her now, standing under the budding branches
> of the grey trees, over which a tinge of green seemed to
> be deepening day after day, her sun-bonnet fallen back
> on her neck, her hands full of delicate wood-flowers, quite
> unconscious of my gaze, but intent on sweet mockery of
> some bird in neighbouring bush or tree. She had the art
> of warbling, and replying to the notes of different birds,
> and knew their song, their habits and ways, more accurately
> than any one else I ever knew. She had often done it at
> my request the spring before; but this year she really
> gurgled, and whistled, and warbled, just as they did, out
> of the very fulness and joy of her heart. She was more
> than ever the very apple of her father's eye; her mother
> gave her both her own share of love and that of the dead
> child who had died in infancy. I have heard cousin Hol-
> man murmur, after a long dreamy look at Phillis, and tell
> herself how like she was growing to Johnnie, and soothe
> herself with plaintive inarticulate sounds, and many gentle
> shakes of the head, for the aching sense of loss she would
> never get over in this world.

My eyes, to be sure, are not what they were: but to
them the prose of this shimmers with beauty. In Mrs.

Gaskell, as with many another ageing writer, one can detect towards the close a certain sunset softness—a haze, we may call it—in which many hard experiences are reconciled. To take the highest, we agree that it so happened to Shakespeare. To step down to the man with whom for a study in the differences of literary genius starting from a like incentive—the woes of the poor, and operating in the same literary form, the novel —I have been—I hope, Gentlemen, not whimsically— contrasting this very noble lady, we know that in his later days, in *Endymion*, Disraeli saw his youth so, casting back to it. And you, maybe, will say that these sunset softening colours are all a mirage. Well, a great deal of it all is that. I believe that, as you grow older, you will find yourselves more and more tending to make less, and still less, account of definitions, of sharp outlines and judgments based on them; of anybody's positive assertions, be he never so young.

IX

I have been speaking, however, to-day of one whose measure in any light has never to my thinking been accurately taken. The crew of Odysseus were Greeks. They beached their ship (says Homer) on the isle of the Laestrygonians: and there came down to them the Queen of the Laestrygonians, "a woman as tall as a mountain," *and they hated her.* The Victorian Age lent itself to excess; and its excessive figures are our statues for some to deface or bedaub. But I, who have purposely compared Elizabeth Gaskell with her most ornate contemporary, dare to prophesy that when criticism has sifted all out, she will come to her own, as a woman of genius, sweetly proportioned as a statue, yet breathing; one of these writers we call by that vain word—so vain, so pathetic even when used of the greatest poet—"immortal."

ANTHONY TROLLOPE

THE BARSETSHIRE NOVELS

I

A FEW months ago I asked a publisher if he had
ever thought of venturing on a complete edition
of Trollope, and was answered that he had thought of
it often, but doubted it would not pay. A few weeks
ago I referred this answer to an eminent bookseller, and
he praised the publisher's judgment. I retain my
belief that the pair of them are mistaken: for let the
name of Trollope be mentioned in any company of
novel-lovers, almost to a certainty one or two will
kindle, avow a passion for him, and start a chorus of
lament that there exists no complete worthy edition of
him.

"All Balzac's novels occupy one shelf"—and all
Trollope's would occupy a plaguey long one. Some
of them, too, are hasty, baddish novels. None the less,
I see that shelf as one of trusted and familiar resort
for such a number of my fellows as would fill a respect-
able subscription-list: and, anyhow, it remains a scandal
that certain good works of his—*The Eustace Diamonds*,
for instance—are unprocurable save by advertising for
second-hand copies. Mr. Humphrey Milford, of the
Oxford University Press, has recently printed *The
Claverings* and *The Belton Estate* in the World's Classics,

with the *Autobiography*, which did, as it happened, about as much harm as a perfectly honest book could do to an honest man's fame. Messrs. Chatto & Windus —whom, as Cicero would say, "I name for the sake of honour," as publishers who respect their moral contract to keep an author's books alive while they can—have kept on sale some eight or nine, including *The American Senator*, *The Way We Live Now*, and *The Golden Lion of Grandpré;* and the famous Barsetshire six, of which Messrs. George Bell now offer us a cheap and pleasant reprint,[1] have always been (as they say in Barset) "come-at-able" in some form or another. But while three full editions of Stevenson have been subscribed for since his death in 1894 (the first of them fetching far more than the original price), and his sale in cheaper editions has been high and constant, Trollope, who died in 1882, has, in these forty-odd years, received no gratitude of public recognition at all answerable to his deserts.

It is a curious business in two ways. For the first, the rebirth of Trollope's fame, with the growing readiness of an admirer to cast away apology and hail a fellow-admirer as a friend "by adoption tried," has nothing esoteric about it. A passion for Peacock, or for Landor—as a passion for Pindar—you may share with a friend as a half-masonic, half-amorous secret. But there can be no such freemasonry over Trollope, who is as English as a cut off the joint or a volume of *Punch*. For the second curiosity, I suppose that no man ever wrote himself down at a more delicately ill-

---

[1] Trollope's Barsetshire Novels: (1) *The Warden*, (2) *Barchester Towers*, (3) *Dr. Thorne*, (4) *Framley Parsonage*, (5) *The Small House at Allington* (2 vols.), (6) *The Last Chronicle of Barset* (2 vols.) 8 vols. 25*s*. the set.   (Bell & Sons.)

chosen time than did Trollope by the publication
(posthumous) of his *Autobiography* in 1883. It was a
brave—if unconsciously brave—and candid book.
But it fell on a generation of young men fired in literature by Flaubert, in painting (say) by Whistler; on a
generation just beginning to be flamboyant over "art
for art's sake," the *mot juste*, and the rest. It all seems
vain enough at this distance, and the bigots of each successive iron time will always be arraigning their fathers'
harmless art, no doubt to the ultimate advancement of
letters. But by young men quite honestly and freneti-
cally devoted to chiselling out English as though (God
rest them!) in obedience to a Higher Power, it may be
allowed that such a confession as the following would
be felt as an irritant:

All those, I think, who have lived as literary men—
working daily as literary labourers—will agree with me that
three hours a day will produce as much as a man ought to
write. But then he should so have trained himself that he
shall be able to work continuously during those three hours
—or have so tutored his mind that it shall not be necessary
for him to sit nibbling his pen and gazing at the wall before
him till he shall have found the words with which he wants
to express his ideas. It had at this time become my custom—and it still is my custom, though of late I have become a little lenient to myself—to write with my watch
before me, and to require from myself 250 words every
quarter of an hour. I have found that my 250 words have
been forthcoming as regularly as my watch went.

The reader may easily imagine the maddening effect
of that upon any ambitious young writer, indolent by
habit yet conscientious in his craft, reminiscent of
hours spent in gazing at a wall for words with which he

wanted to express his ideas. How many times did Plato alter the opening sentence of *The Republic?* How many times did Gray recast the *Elegy?*

But time, which should bring the philosophic mind, will lead most critics who follow criticism sincerely to the happy conviction that there are no rules for the operation of genius; a conviction born to save a vast amount of explanation—and whitewash. Literary genius may be devoted, as with Milton; nonchalant, as with Congreve; elaborately draped, as with Tennyson. Catullus or Burns may splash your face and run on; but always the unmistakable god has passed your way. In reading Trollope one's sense of trafficking with genius arises more and more evidently out of his large sincerity—a sincerity in bulk, so to speak; wherefore, to appraise him, you must read him in bulk, taking the good with the bad, even as you must with Shakespeare. (This comparison is not so foolish as it looks at first sight: since, while no two authors can ever have been more differently gifted, it would be difficult to name a third in competition as typically English.) The very mass of Trollope commands a real respect; its prodigious quantity is felt to be a quality, as one searches in it and finds that—good or bad, better or very much worse—there is not a dishonest inch in the whole. He practised among novelists of genius: Dickens, Thackeray, Disraeli, the Brontës, George Eliot, Ouida were his contemporaries; he lived through the era of "sensational novels," *Lady Audley's Secret* and the rest; and he wrote, as he confesses, with an eye on the publisher's cheque. But no success of genius tempted him to do more than admire it from a distance; no success of "sensation" seduced him from his loom of honest tweed. He criticises the gods and Titans of his time.

He had personal reasons for loving Thackeray, who gave him his great lift into fame by commissioning him to write the serial novel that opened the *Cornhill* upon a highly expectant public. Trollope played up nobly to the compliment and the responsibility. *Framley Parsonage* belongs to his very best: it took the public accurately (and deservedly) between wind and water. Thackeray was grateful for the good and timely service; Trollope for the good and timely opportunity. Yet one suspects no taint of servility when he writes of Thackeray that "among all our novelists his style is the purest, as to my ear it is the most harmonious." (And so, I hope, say most of us.) Of Dickens he declares with entire simplicity that his "own peculiar idiosyncrasy in the matter" forbids him to join in the full chorus of applause. "Mrs. Gamp, Micawber, Pecksniff, and others have become household words—but to my judgment they are not human beings."

Of Dickens's style it is impossible to speak in praise. It is jerky, ungrammatical, and created by himself in defiance of rules—almost as completely as that created by Carlyle. To readers who have taught themselves to regard language, it must therefore be unpleasant. But the critic is driven to feel the weakness of his criticism when he acknowledges to himself—as he is compelled in all honesty to do—that with the language, such as it is, the writer has satisfied the great mass of the readers of his country.

To the merits of Disraeli—whom he must take into account as "the present Prime Minister of England," who "has been so popular as a novelist that, whether for good or for ill, I feel myself compelled to speak of him"—he is quite genuinely blind. For the political insight which burns in page after page of *Coningsby*, as

for the seriousness at the core of *Sybil*, he has no eyes
at all. To him, dealing with the honest surface and
sub-surface of English country life, with the rooted
interest of county families and cathedral closes, all
Disraeli's pictures of high society appear as pomatum
and tinsel, false glitter and flash. He had never a
guess that this flash and glitter (false as they so often
were) played over depths his own comfortable philosophy never divined. He just found it false and denounced it. Upon Wilkie Collins and the art that
constructed *The Woman in White* and *The Moonstone*
he could only comment that "as it is a branch which
I have not myself at all cultivated, it is not unnatural
that his work should be very much lost upon me
individually. When I sit down to write a novel I do
not at all know, and I do not very much care, how it is
to end."

Again, honest though he was, he accepted and used
false tricks and conventions calculated, in the 'eighties
and 'nineties, to awake frenzy in any young practitioner
who, however incompetent, was trying to learn how a
novel should be written. The worst "stage aside" of
an old drama was as nothing in comparison with
Trollope's easy-going remarks, dropped anywhere in
the story, and anyhow, that "This is a novel, and I am
writing it to amuse you. I might just as easily make
my heroine do *this* as do *that*. Which shall it be? . . .
Well, I am going to make her do *that;* for if she did
this, what would become of my novel?" One can
imagine Henry James wincing physically at such a
question posed in cold print by an artist; as in a most
catholic and charitable paper—written in 1883, when
the young dogs were assembling to insult Trollope's
carcase—he reveals himself as wincing over the first

sentence in the last chapter of *Barchester Towers:*
"The end of a novel, like the end of a children's dinner-
party, must be made up of sweetmeats and sugar
plums." James laments:

These little slaps at credulity . . . are very discourag-
ing, but they are even more inexplicable; for they are
deliberately inartistic, even judged from the point of view
of that rather vague consideration of form which is the
only canon we have a right to impose upon Trollope. It
is impossible to imagine what a novelist takes himself to
be unless he regard himself as a historian and his narrative
as history. It is only as a historian that he has the smallest
locus standi. As a narrator of fictitious events he is nowhere;
to insert into his attempt a backbone of logic he must relate
events that are assumed to be real. This assumption
permeates, animates all the work of the most solid story-
tellers. . . .

Yes; but on further acquaintance with Trollope one
discovers that this trick (annoying always) of asking,
"Now what shall we make Mrs. Bold do?—accept
Mr. Arabin, or reject him?" is no worse than "uncle's
fun," as I may put it. Uncle is just playing with us,
though we wish he wouldn't. In fact, Trollope never
chooses the wrong answer to the infelicitous question.
He is wise and unerringly right every time. You will
(I think) search his novels in vain for a good man or
a good woman untrue to duty as weighed out between
heart and conscience.

Another offence in Trollope is his distressing employment of facetious names—"Mr. Quiverful" for a
philoprogenitive clergyman, "Dr. Fillgrave" for a
family physician, etc. "It would be better," murmurs
Henry James pathetically, "to go back to Bunyan at

once." (Trollope, in fact, goes back farther—to the
abominable tradition of Ben Jonson; and it is the less
excusable because he could invent perfect names when
he tried—Archdeacon Grantly, Johnny Eames, Algernon Crosbie, Mrs. Proudie, the Dales of Allington, the
Thornes of Ullathorne, Barchester, Framley—names,
families, places fitting like gloves.) And still worse was
he advised when he introduced caricature, for which
he had small gift, into his stories; "taking off" eminent
bishops in the disguise of objectionable small boys, or
poking laborious fun at Dickens and Carlyle under the
titles of Mr. Sentiment and Dr. Pessimist Anticant.
The Warden is in conception, and largely in execution,
a beautiful story of an old man's conscience. It is a
short story, too. I know of none that could be more
easily shortened to an absolute masterpiece by a pair of
scissors.

With Trollope, as with Byron, in these days a critic
finds himself at first insensibly forced, as though by
shouldering of a crowd, upon apology for the man's
reputation.

II

I do not wish to make a third with Pontius Pilate
and Mr. Chadband in raising the question, "What is
Truth?" but merely to suggest here that, as soon as
ever you raise it over poetry or over prose fiction, it
becomes—as Aristotle did not miss to discover—highly
philosophical and ticklish. To begin at plumb bottom
with your mere matter-of-fact man, you will be asked
to explain how in the world there can be "truth" in
"fiction," the two being opponent and mutually ex-
clusive terms; and such a man will tell you that lark-
spurs don't listen, lilies don't whisper, and no spray

blossoms with pleasure because a bird has clung to it; wherefore, what is the use of pretending any such lies? Ascending a little higher in the scale of creation, we come to another bottom, a false bottom, a Bully Bottom, who enjoys make-believe, but feels it will never do "to bring in (God shield us!) a lion among ladies." Still ascending past much timber, we emerge on the decks of argosies—

> Like signiors and rich burghers on the flood,

portlily negligent of all this bottom-business on which they ride, carrying piled canvas over the foam of perilous seas. In short, the man who hasn't it in his soul that there is a truth of emotion and a truth of imagination just as solid for a keelson as any truth of fact, merely does not know what literature is *about*. As Heine once said of a fat opponent, "it is easier for a camel to enter the Kingdom of Heaven than for that fellow to pass through the eye of a needle." Now Trollope, if we look at him in one way, and consider him as an entirely honest Bottom, simply saw Micawber as a grotesque creation and Victor Hugo as a writer extravagantly untrue to nature. He merely could not understand what Hugo would be aiming at (say) in *Gastibelza* or in the divine serenade:

> Allons-nous-en par l'Autriche!
>   Nous aurons l'aube à nos fronts.
> Je serai grand et toi riche,
>   Puisque nous nous aimerons . . .
>
> Tu seras dame et moi comte.
>   Viens, mon cœur s'épanouit.
> Viens, nous conterons ce conte
>   Aux étoiles de la nuit.

He could as little see—and yet who doubts it?—that
the creator of Micawber was absolutely honest in
closing *David Copperfield* on the declaration that "no
one can ever believe this Narrative in the reading
more than I believed it in the writing." What Trollope
made of *Don Quixote* (or of *Alice in Wonderland*) lies
beyond my power to imagine. But the point for us is
that as an honest man who lived through the vogue
of Poe and Dickens and, in later times, of Ouida (who
will surely, soon or late, be recognised for the genius
she was), and was all the time, on his own admission,
alive as anyone to the market, Trollope kept the noise-
less tenor of his way and, resisting temptation this side
or that, went on describing life as he saw it.

Thus, and in this easy, humdrum, but pertinacious
style, he arrived, much as he often arrived at the death
of a fox. He was a great fox-hunter; lumbering in the
saddle, heavy, short-sighted, always unaware of what
might happen on t'other side of the next fence—"few
have explored more closely than I have done the depth
and breadth and water-holding capacities of an Essex
ditch." He knew little of the science of the sport:

Indeed, all the notice I take of hounds is not to ride
over them. My eyes are so constituted that I can never
see the nature of a fence. I either follow some one, or
ride at it with the full conviction that I may be going into
a horse-pond or a gravel-pit. I have jumped into both one
and the other. I am very heavy and have never ridden
expensive horses.

"The cause of my delight in the amusement," he confesses, "I have never been able to analyze to my own
satisfaction." He arose regularly at 5:30 A.M., had his
coffee brought him by a groom, had completed his

"literary work" before he dressed for breakfast; then on four working days a week he toiled for the General Post Office, and on the other two rode to hounds. In all kinds of spare time—in railway-carriages or crossing to America—he had always a pen in his hand, a pad of paper on his knee, or on a cabin table specially constructed.

As he sets it all down, with parenthetical advice to the literary tyro, it is all as simple, apparently, as a cash account. But don't you believe it! The man who created the Barsetshire novels lived quite as intimately with his theme as Dickens did in *David Copperfield;* nay, more intimately. To begin with, his imaginary Barsetshire is as definitely an actual piece of England as Mr. Hardy's Wessex. Of *Framley Parsonage* he tells us that

as I wrote it I became more closely than ever acquainted with the new shire which I had added to the English counties. . . . I had it all in my mind—its roads and railroads, its towns and parishes, its members of Parliament and the different hunts that rode over it. I knew all the great lords and their castles, the squires and their parks, the rectors and their churches. This was the fourth novel of which I had placed the scene in Barsetshire, and as I wrote it I made a map of the dear county. Throughout these stories there has been no name given to a fictitious site which does not represent to me a spot of which I know all the accessories, as though I had lived and wandered there.

Here Trollope asserts less than one-half of his true claim. He not only carried all Barsetshire in his brain as a map, with every cross-road, by-lane, and footpath noted—Trollope was great at cross-roads, having as an official reorganised, simplified, and speeded-up the postal service over a great part of rural England—but knew all the country-houses, small or great, of that shire, with their families, pedigrees, intermarriages, political interests, monetary anxieties, the rise and fall of interdependent squires, parsons, tenants; how a mortgage, for example, will influence a character, a bank-book set going a matrimonial intrigue, a transferred bill operate on a man's sense of honour. You seem to see him moving about the Cathedral Close in "very serviceable suit of black," or passing the gates and lodge of a grand house in old hunting-pink like a very wise solicitor on a holiday: garrulous, to be sure, but to be trusted with any secret—to be trusted most of all, perhaps, with that secret of a maiden's love which as yet she hardly dares to avow to herself. Here let us listen to the late Frederic Harrison, who puts it exactly:

The Barsetshire cycle of tales has one remarkable feature; for it is designed[1] on a scheme which is either a delightful success or a tiresome failure. And it is a real success. To fill eight volumes in six distinct tales with the intricate relations of one set of families, all within access to one cathedral city, covering a whole generation in time, and exhibiting the same characters from youth to maturity and age—this is indeed a perilous task. . . . Balzac and Zola abroad have done this, and with us Scott, Thackeray, Lytton, and Dickens have in some degree tried this plan. But, I think, no English novelist has worked it out on so large a field, with such minute elaboration, and with such entire mastery of the many dilemmas and pitfalls which beset the competitor in this long and intricate course.

It is a strange reflection—as one turns the advertisement pages of *The Times*, or of *Country Life*, and scans

[1] I should prefer to say that it grew.—Q.

the photographs of innumerable "stately homes" to-day on the market—that Trollope's fame should be reviving just as the society he depicted would seem to be in process of deracination. I use the word "deracination" because that society—with all its faults, stunted offshoots, gnarled prejudices, mossed growth of convention, parasitic ivies—was a tree of ancestry rooted in the countryside, not to be extracted save by wrenching of fibres and with bleeding of infinite homely ties. To some extent, no doubt, this sorrowful dislocation must follow all long wars. A hundred years ago Cobbett rode our land and noted how its true gentry, as a reward for their very sacrifices during the Napoleonic struggle, were being dispossessed by bankers and "loan-mongers." So, to-day, are decent families— who, while "thinking too much of themselves," thought much for their neighbours—being uprooted and exiled, and taking into lodgings a few portraits, some medals, and the last framed piece of vellum conferring posthumously a D.S.O. *These* times, at any rate, do not "strike monied worldlings with dismay." On the contrary, the war-profiteer and the week-ender with his golf-clubs are smothering the poor last of the society that Trollope knew; and in time, no doubt, *their* sons will go to Eton and Winchester, learn in holidays the old English love of field and stream and sea, and so prepare themselves in a generation or two to cast off life at earliest call simply because this England, to which they have succeeded, has come to be, in *their* turn, *their* country. Thus it will go on again (please heaven) as the father's hair wears off the grandson's hoof.

The fortunes and misfortunes of Trollope's comfortable England have always this element of the universal, that they are not brought about by any

devastating external calamity, but always by process of
inward rectitude or inward folly, reasonably operating
on the ordinary business of life.　In this business he
can win and keep our affection for an entirely good
man—for Mr. Harding, for Doctor Thorne.　In all his
treatment of women, even of the *jeune fille* of the
Victorian Age, this lumbering, myopic rider-to-hounds
always (as they say) "has hands"—and to "have
hands" is a gift of God.　He was, as Henry James
noted, "by no means destitute of a certain saving grace
of coarseness," but it is forgotten on the instant he
touches a woman's pulse.　Over that, to interpret it,
he never bends but delicately.　No one challenges his
portraits of the maturer ladies.　Mrs. Proudie is a
masterpiece, of course, heroically consistent to the
moment of her death—nay, living afterwards con-
sistently in her husband's qualified regrets (can anything be truer than the tragedy told with complete
restraint in chapters 66 and 67 of *The Last Chronicle*?).
Lady Lufton's portrait, while less majestic, seems to me
equally flawless, equally flawless.　Trollope's women
can all show claws on occasion; can all summon "that
sort of ill-nature which is not uncommon when one
woman speaks of another"; and the most, even of his
maidens, betray sooner or later some glance of that
malice upon the priestly calling, or rather upon its
pretensions, which Trollope made them share with him:

"Ah! yes: but Lady Lufton is not a clergyman, Miss
Robarts."
It was on Lucy's tongue to say that her ladyship was
pretty nearly as bad, but she stopped herself.

Difference of time and convention and pruderies
allowed for, Trollope will give you in a page or so of

discourse between two Victorian maidens—the whole
of it delicately understood, chivalrously handled,
tenderly yet firmly revealed—the secret as no novelist
has quite revealed it before or since. At any moment
one may be surprised by a sudden Jane Austen touch;
and this will come with the more startling surprise
being dropped by a plain, presumably blunt, man.
For Trollope adds to his strain of coarseness, already
mentioned, a strain—or at least an intimate understanding—of cheapness. His gentle breeding and his
upbringing (poverty-stricken though it had been) ever
checked him on the threshold of the holies. But he
had tholed too many years in the G.P.O. to have
missed intimate acquaintance with

> The noisy chaff
> And ill-bred laugh
> Of clerks on omnibuses.

Those who understand this will understand why he
could not bring himself to mate his "dear Lily Dale"
with that faithful, most helpful, little bounder Johnny
Eames. He knew his Johnny Eames too well to introduce him upon the Cathedral Close of Barchester,
though he could successfully dare to introduce the
Stanhope family. He walks among rogues, too, and
wastrels, with a Mr. Sowerby or a Bertie Stanhope, as
sympathetically as among bishops, deans, archdeacons,
canons. His picture of Sowerby and the ruin he has
brought on an ancient family, all through his own sins
is no less and no more truthful than his picture of Mrs.
Proudie in altercation with Mr. Slope; while they both
are inferior in imaginative power to the scene of Mr.
Crawley's call on the Bishop. In the invention of

Crawley, in his perfect handling of that strong and insane mind, I protest that I am astonished almost as though he had suddenly shown himself capable of inventing a King Lear. In this Trollope, with whom one has been jogging along under a slowly growing conviction that he is by miles a greater artist than he knows or has ever been reckoned, there explodes this character—and out of the kindliest intentions to preach him up, one is awakened in a fright and to a sense of shame at never having recognised the man's originality or taken the great measure of his power.

INDEX